ARE YOUR KIDS NAKED ONLINE?

ARE YOUR KIDS NAKED ONLINE?

How to protect your tech-savvy kids from online self-destruction

Chris Good & Lisa Good

Download The Parenting Technology Toolkit For FREE!

READ THIS FIRST

Just to say thanks for reading our book, we would like to give you The Parenting Technology Toolkit that contains additional resources to help you on your quest to protect your kids online absolutely FREE. *-Chris Good & Lisa Good*

To register your book go to:

www.AreYourKidsNakedOnline.com/registerbook

TABLE OF CONTENTS

INTRODUCTION

The Why Behind The Book

Wow, we bet you are wondering why in the world anyone would title a book, *Are Your Kids* **Naked** *Online?* Well, it did grab your attention, right? Just the word "naked" invokes a head-turning reaction with pretty much everyone, no matter what your political or religious beliefs. Everyone from all walks of life knows the basic meaning of "naked," which is unclothed or bare. In addition, in the world we live in today, just about everyone has heard of someone, whether it's a friend's child, a family member's child, a co-worker's child, or some celebrity, having nude photos show up online, whether intentional or leaked.

However, naked means more than just "unclothed." Some of the synonyms for naked are: unprotected, uncovered, exposed, unguarded, vulnerable, helpless, weak, powerless, defenseless, and open to attack.[1]

This book is about much more than naked photos of your children showing up online. When we say "naked online," we are also referring to the following:

- Naked—Ignorant: Not knowledgeable about the real dangers when it comes to social media, chats, the dark web, and online gaming

- Naked—Defenseless: No protective mechanisms in place to help prevent or detect problems, both physical (monitoring tools, parental controls) and mental

- Naked—Unprotected: Parent or other adults not involved and engaged in teaching, positive communication, ongoing dialogue, and support

- Naked—Vulnerable: Sharing private information that can endanger their lives and possibly even expose them to predators

- Naked—Powerless: Feeling like there is nowhere to go when something is wrong and that their parents will just yell and scream at them

- Naked—Helpless: Feeling like no one would understand them and they would be judged by the adults in their lives for their carelessness

- Naked—Unguarded: Not able to see the consequences or think of the long-term consequences of their decisions

- Naked—Bare: Sending inappropriate photos, videos, or text messages that can open them up to criminal charges, predators, and sex trafficking

Most children today know more than their parents when it comes to technology. However, just because they are tech-savvy doesn't mean they are wise. The majority of kids today are young and immature. If we are all honest, we will remember that when we were young, we weren't all that "wise" either. Lisa Good, one of the authors of this book, recently gave a speech at NASDAQ where she talked about drag racing when she was sixteen years old and having her car taken away and sold. That sounds crazy and reckless, right? Yes, it was—especially for someone who was an "A" student, never got in trouble, and didn't "break" the rules. Even the smartest, most "mature" kids make some unwise decisions. It comes with the territory of being a child. Sometimes their emotions get the best of them, like what happened with Lisa, or just the lack of age that brings experience and wisdom gets the best of them. But in the online digital world we live in today, those emotions and mistakes can have life-altering repercussions. The stakes are high.

Why in the world did we write this book? After all, we work with businesses managing their computer networks, security, and technology infrastructure; consulting on new technology projects; providing compliance and security audits; minimizing their technology risk; and protecting their technology assets. We aren't psychologists or school counselors.

In addition to our technical expertise, we are also parents of four (just four) children, two sons and two daughters, who at the time of this writing are all teenagers.

In our twenty-plus years of business, we have had the privilege of working with entrepreneurs, politicians, celebrities, and business owners in every industry and of every size. The one commonality between them all is we often found ourselves sitting across from them having a very serious conversation—a conversation that had nothing to do with their business technology and everything to do with their children, their nieces, nephews, or grandchildren and technology.

Some of those conversations were heart-breaking.

"She sent an inappropriate picture to her boyfriend and he shared it with the entire football team. She tried to commit suicide. Is there any way to get those photos back?"

"He was at a party after the senior prom and some friends talked him into smoking weed. Photos were posted online, and now the college wants to rescind his scholarship. We can't afford to send him without that scholarship."

"My daughter and her best friend had a disagreement and they both said some things online while angry. The school suspended my daughter and is considering expelling her. The school said that what she posted was considered bullying, and they have a zero tolerance policy. They don't care about the context or what her friend wrote. She is only in seventh grade. This could ruin her future."

"My son and his friends were looking at pornography on his school laptop. He's been suspended from school and the police have been called. Apparently, there are pornographic images of children on his laptop."

Other conversations felt more like covert Q&A sessions.

"Is there a way to put a tracking device on my daughter's phone without her knowing or finding it? She says she's going to the library, but she never brings home any books."

"Can I have the web camera on my son's computer set up to record when my son's friends come over without the light glowing or them noticing that it's on? I think they may be smoking weed in the house."

"My son posted something incredibly dumb on Instagram, should I call him out publicly and post my response? Or, how do I get him to remove it completely?"

Through every conversation, we applied the same principles we used to tackle their business technology issues on their super-smart, tech-savvy children's technology issues, except for one thing: we were parents, too. While our children hadn't made the mistakes some of their children had, we knew they weren't infallible, and we could imagine the heartbreak these parents were going through.

Those conversations and promptings from clients to help other parents they knew are what brought this book to life.

We aren't perfect parents, but we love our children, and we know other parents love their children as well. We do not know of a single parent that would consider sending their child naked to school or to the mall, yet how often are children being sent naked into the online digital world? No parent wants their child to suffer because of a foolish mistake, but yet our children and all the children growing up in this new digital world are held to that standard. We are IT and security experts, who are also parents, who want to help you protect your children from online self-destruction.

This book is designed to provide you with the basic knowledge of today's digital landscape in which children live. It is also designed to provide suggestions, tips, and tools to help you protect your child, or children—if you are like us and have more than one. We know that sometimes things slip out of control. Maybe you never set rules or boundaries, and now you are seeing negative behavior that is concerning. Or perhaps your child may have already made some mistakes with their cell phone. Many chapters in this book have a "What You Can Do" section at the end with tips and suggestions.

While we can't cover every possible situation you may

encounter, we have tried to cover the most common ones.

Remember, you are preparing your children to be independent thinkers and problem solvers. No parent wants their children to be twenty-somethings who need a parent to hold their hand every step of adulthood or are still living at home in the basement on their computer all day playing games in their underwear. The teaching and training you do now will help your child make good decisions on their own when they leave and become responsible, connected citizens of this digital world.

With a little bit of guidance, many conversations, and a lot of prayers, it is our hope that your children can thrive, flourish, and succeed in this digital world in which they live without catastrophic consequences and with their future bright and intact.

CHAPTER 1

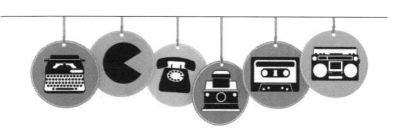

Times Have Changed

Times certainly have changed since we were kids. Sure, we had computers, but what we had, we had to program. Does anyone remember the first Commodore 64 or Apple computers? What about the first computer that ran in DOS or Windows 3.1? You certainly weren't taking those computers to your friend's house for the afternoon! The laptops that were out at that time were primarily used by NASA and the military.

None of us knew anything about hacking and the internet as we know it today did not exist. Prior to 1991,[2] the "internet" was only primarily used by those in the education and government sectors, as well as the military.

Cell phones...hmm, when we were younger, the only people who had cell phones were politicians, high-ranking military officials, lawyers and celebrities. I'm not sure that even celebrities had cell phones. And when I say "cell phones," I'm talking about those huge things usually shaped like bricks in your car that looked like an extension of your home telephone, curly line and all. You didn't see people walking around the grocery store talking on a phone and you certainly couldn't "text" a message to pick up bread while you were at the store—texting did not exist. In fact, in the late 1980s, cell phones were still an extravagance, and by 1990 only 4 percent of Americans had a cell phone. Smartphones didn't even hit the market until 2005.

If you haven't guessed by now, we were born in the 1970s. (Our kids like to say, "in the Jurassic Era"—I can hear my parents snickering now...)

Our kids look at us shocked and then laugh when we tell them what it was like growing up, way back then.

"You had no cell phone? What did you do when you were at the grocery store and couldn't remember something? What, you had to have a written list? If you forgot something you had to walk back? Seriously?!? How did you tell your friends that you were going to go to the movies? What, you had to preplan everything and stick to the plan? What if you changed your mind? You had to buy cassette tapes or records for music? There was no streaming or iTunes? What *did you do* for fun?"

It's almost like they think we lived in a cave, sat around, and picked our teeth with dinosaur bones!

The advancement of technology has been great. Seriously, I cannot imagine going to the grocery store without my "smart" phone! All the moms reading this are nodding their heads in agreement. However, that advancement has brought along dangers which we as parents never had to deal with—dangers that did not exist when we were kids, and dangers that can have serious consequences. And I don't mean the kind where you were at a party on Friday night and drank too much and now everyone at school on Monday is going to laugh at you for vomiting all over the place.

The dangers our kids face today with technology are life-changing and can be life ending. The rate of drug overdose and addiction, thanks in part to kids being able to purchase drugs on the dark web online anonymously, has doubled since 2015,[3] according to the U.S. Centers for Disease Control and Prevention, while suicide for kids between the ages of ten and twenty-four has tripled since 2015.[4] It is no surprise that those statistics coincide with the 24/7/365 online life that consumes our kids today.

While every generation has encountered and dealt with peer pressure, bullying, and child predators, the social media world that our children live in today has taken these three matters to an unprecedented level. Prior to social media, when kids had a disagreement or a fight with a friend, they might share it with another close friend and their parents. They would go home, sleep on things, have time to let the dust settle, so to speak, and then, most times, they would work things out or come to some type of understanding.

In today's digital world, both parties involved will be posting, tweeting, and sharing their side of the story in the heat of the moment with whatever words they want to type. Every one of their friends, followers, and peers will know what was said between them, whether in person, through text, or on social media. They may even include screenshots of text messages and post audio or video of their disagreement, anything that will help them win the battle on social media in that moment.

Unfortunately, most times what began as a simple misunderstanding, which could have been cleared up if both parties would have had some time to think about what really happened, turns into a friendship-ending event and—even worse—becomes a bitter grudge. Neither child wants to look foolish or be perceived as wrong on social media to their friends or followers. If they share the same group of friends, their friends now feel obligated to pick sides. It is a vicious cycle that can have deadly consequences. Suicides from online shaming, bullying, and fights are on the rise.

Now, we are not going to tell you that you should pull your kids off the internet or take their computers and iPhones away, even though for some parents (and their children), that would be the best course of action. However, for most parents today, that point in time has passed. What we will tell you is that you can protect your kids in today's digital world, even though your kids are way smarter than you about today's technology and the digital world in which we now live. Some things may not be easy, but our job as parents isn't supposed to be easy.

It starts with open, honest, and frank discussions with your children. You also need to be aware and involved as a parent. You may say, "I have teens" or "It's too late." To that we say, it's never too late! It may be a bit more challenging depending on your relationship with your child, but if they are still alive, it is *not* too late.

The "Just Say No" and D.A.R.E. campaigns against drugs were failures. Even though the intentions were good, there are facts and data[5] to prove that they were not successful. While technology itself is not a drug, studies[6] show that the way a person's brain reacts to the internet, specifically social media, is similar to the way one with a substance use disorder reacts to stimulation from drugs. The same dopamine spike that people with real drug and alcohol addictions experience is happening to our children who are living their lives 24/7/365 on the internet and social media.

Did you know that social media and its addictive behavior doesn't just affect behavior during the day? According to the Trends in Consumer Mobility Report,[7] which studies consumers' behaviors toward gadgets, approximately 71 percent of Americans sleep with or next to their cell phones, with 55 percent of those being teenagers. About 10 percent of teens check their phones more than ten times per night for social media updates. Is it any wonder why children today are drinking four and five Monster energy drinks or Starbucks just to make it through their day?

For most parents in today's age, it is not realistic to take a "just say no" approach with their children and technology. Most kids cannot just "say no to technology"; 90 percent[8] of all jobs today require some knowledge of technology. What we can and should be doing as parents is talking about what can happen when we use technology in the wrong ways, the dangers that exist with technology, and how the internet is not all rainbows and unicorns—it's not a 100 percent safe place.

Just like we teach our kids about talking to strangers, being aware of their surroundings, looking both ways before crossing the street, and being careful of the friends with whom they hang out, these same lessons and basic principles need to be applied and taught for technology use. We can limit the age at which they get technology and begin using technology. We can also limit the use of technology in our homes—after all, it's your home, your rules. (Oh, my, I just sounded like my father....)

While schools have incorporated lessons on technology, they can't possibly cover everything, and the reality is, as a parent it is *your responsibility* to teach and protect your child (or children) from the dangers of technology.

If you still don't think it's important to teach your kids about internet safety, here are a few statistics:

- One in ten kids under age ten have seen pornography online.[9]

- Pornography searches increase by 4,700 percent when kids are using the internet in the hours after school ends.[9]

- Children under the age of ten account for 22 percent of online porn consumption for the age group of children zero to eighteen years old.[9]

- Forty-four percent of kids ages eight to sixteen years old have hidden their online activity from their parents, and the proportion increases as kids get older.[10]

- Seventy percent of parents whose kids have hidden their online activity are unaware of what their kids are doing on the internet.[10]

- Thirteen percent of kids have accessed inappropriate content when their parents were not at home.[10]

- Twenty-two percent said they have used anonymizers, or anonymous proxy tools, to make their internet activity untraceable.[10]

- Fourteen percent reported that they downloaded applications that hid the apps they open.[10]

- One in seven children between the ages of twelve and seventeen have sent a "sext" (naked photo).[11]

- One in four children between the ages of twelve and seventeen have received a "sext" (naked photo).[11]

When working with a business, we look at protecting clients like the layers of an onion. Each device or service used to protect the client adds an additional layer of protection to the business, and the more layers you have, the greater the protection. As a parent, you also need to look at protecting your children just like the layers of an onion. The more layers you have, the better your child will be protected. With your children, there are two main types or layers of protection.

The first type of protection is the physical layer. Just like you have locks on the doors, an alarm system, and smoke/fire alarms at your home or business, the equivalent for today's parent is monitoring software, parental controls, a business-grade firewall that your tech-savvy kids and their friends can't get past (or would take them a lot of effort to bypass), online reports, etc.

The second type of protection would be the communication and mental layer. This includes ongoing open communication, education of digital dangers, teaching appropriate online use, and the most critical: building a bond of trust so that when something goes wrong, they will come and talk to you or another adult in their life.

Parenting in today's digital world is a new frontier, similar to exploring the deep ocean. There is no map, the terrain changes sometimes without notice, and you never know what can be lurking around the corner. It's best to make sure everyone in the submarine (your home) is prepared.

CHAPTER 2

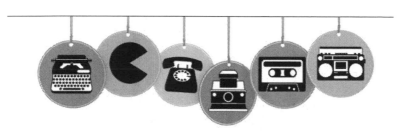

The Lingo of Today's Digital Kids: An Online and Social Media Primer for the Rest of Us

This chapter is just a quick primer of some of the online and social media lingo kids use today. We've also included a brief section of texting acronyms that parents and adults should be familiar with, as well as other beneficial information that really needed to be in one chapter instead of repeated in multiple chapters throughout the book.

We did not include every definition or acronym that kids use today; we only included the ones we thought would be beneficial in the context of this book.

Social Media Platforms of Choice

There are multiple social media platforms today. Your child

may use only one, they may use a few, they may have accounts on all platforms, or they may even have multiple accounts for secret purposes on some of the platforms. As of the writing of this book, the main players are Facebook, Snapchat, Instagram, Twitter, Tumblr, Pinterest, and Google+.

While Facebook is one of the granddaddies of social media, data shows that Facebook is no longer the social media platform of choice for teenagers. So what are they using now? According to Statista, they are using Snapchat and Instagram.

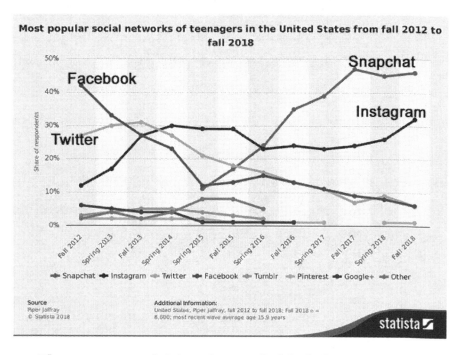

There are two driving factors behind that. One, Instagram and Snapchat make it very easy to set up new "fake" or anonymous accounts that most parents won't know exist. We predict that the use of Instagram will decline over the next several years. Why?

In the fall of 2018, the two founders of Instagram left. There is speculation regarding why, but the consensus is that Facebook, its parent company, was no longer happy to let Instagram do its "own" thing. In the wake of their departure, several Facebook employees have stepped in to take the reins. Rumor in the tech world is that Instagram will incorporate all the rules, features, and checks and balances of Facebook in the upcoming two years. This will make it much harder for kids to create multiple accounts on Instagram. It looks like they are also going to integrate all the advertising that Facebook is famous for into Instagram, so all its users will also get bombarded with ads everywhere they turn.

With regard to Snapchat, besides the ease of creating multiple accounts, the real reason that kids love it and use it heavily is because of the "auto deleting" of messages. Most kids today still believe that their messages are deleted forever, thereby giving them the false impression that what they say, as well as photos and videos they post, will never be seen again, let alone by their parents or other adults in their life.

Basic Terms and Definitions You Should Know

AMA: An acronym for "ask me anything," where users will use the term to prompt questions from other users.

Bunny Hunters: How online predators describe what they do. They pose online as people they're not, sending messages and pictures to innocent "bunnies" (children) in a hunt to lure or coerce them into sexual relationships.

Catfish: Someone who creates a false online identity.

Catfishing: Common on social networking and online dating sites. Sometimes a catfish's sole purpose is to engage in a fantasy. Sometimes, however, the catfish's intent is to defraud a victim, seek revenge, or commit identity theft.

Circumventor Sites: Parallel websites that allow children to get around filtering software and access sites that have been blocked.

Facetune (Facetuned): A photo editing application used to edit, enhance, and retouch photos on a user's iPhone, iPad, or Android device. Often used for portrait and selfie editing. Features allow users to whiten teeth, remove blemishes, smooth skin, reshape, defocus, and blur.

Finsta: A fake Instagram account. A combination of the words "fake" and "Instagram" used to represent someone's hidden, personal second Instagram account used for sharing with a smaller circle of followers.

Free-to-Play Game or App: Does not charge the user or player in order to join the game or use the app. Instead, the company makes money from advertisements or in-game sales, such as payment for upgrades, special abilities, special items, and expansion packs.

Get Down: Sleeping with someone where there are no strings attached. Pre-internet days = one-night stand.

Frenemy: A person with whom one is friendly, despite a fundamental dislike or rivalry. Can also mean a person who combines the characteristics of a friend and an enemy.

Griefers: Internet gamers who intentionally cause problems and/ or cyberbully other gamers (i.e., individuals who play online games).

Hook Up: Also called "hooking up." Any form of intimacy with a member of the preferred sex that you don't consider a significant other. Usually, when said by modern youth, it means to make out and/or have sex with no strings attached. Pre-internet days = one-night stand.

Lurker: A person online who reads discussions on social networks, but rarely or never participates in the discussion. Your children may call *you* a lurker.

Sexting: The sending of nude, partially nude, or sexually suggestive pictures, videos, or text.

Sharenting: The habitual and often overuse of social media by parents to share content about their children. Parents who blog, tweet, and post pictures and details about all aspects of their children's lives.

Social Proof: A psychological phenomenon in which people seek direction from those around them to determine how they are supposed to act or think in a given situation. In social media, social proof is identified by the number of "likes" a piece of content receives or the number of followers you have. The thought is that if others are sharing something or following someone, it must be good.

Troll: A person who is known for creating controversy in an online setting. They typically hang out on social media with the intent of disrupting the conversation by providing commentary that aims to evoke a reaction.

Virtual Reality Devices: The computer-generated simulation in which a person can interact within an artificial three-dimensional environment using special electronic devices, such as special goggles with a screen or gloves fitted with sensors.

A Word About Fake Accounts

It's really easy to create fake accounts on all the social media platforms. All you need is an email address, which doesn't have to be a "real" email address. It can be a Gmail, Hotmail, Yahoo, or any other free email address. Sometimes you will hear them referred to as "throwaway email addresses." People, including kids, use them when they do not want to use an email address that can show their real identity.

It's not uncommon to see kids who have two social media accounts on each platform they use—one that Mom and Dad know about, and one that is private.

Fake accounts are so prevalent that Facebook includes the number of fake accounts it has shut down every quarter on its website[12] and in its financial reports. The number for the third quarter of 2018 is 754 million accounts. That is roughly 251 million fake accounts per month!

Advice About Catfishing

If you believe your child is in a catfishing situation, it is important to make copies of all their communications. This is your proof that something fraudulent happened. Remember, people who catfish will delete the account and everything in it as soon as they think they have been caught. You can also run a reverse image search on Google to see if the photos they have actually belong to someone else.

If you determine that you actually have a catfish situation, be sure to report it to the social media provider, your child's school, and the police. Do not unfriend the person or remove them from your child's account until you have talked with the proper authorities.

Texting and Social Media Acronyms That Should Concern You

There are well over fifty texting and social media acronyms that kids today use. It is their "secret" language. We have included a few below. When you register your book, you'll receive a more comprehensive list of commonly used terms in the Parenting Technology Toolkit.

PIR—Parent in room	**KMS**—Kill myself
PAW—Parents are watching	**@@@**—Warning of parents nearby
KPC—Keeping parents clueless	**DOC**—Drug of choice

GNOC—Get naked on camera	**IWSN**—I want sex now
Netflix and chill—Code for engaging in sex or other sexual acts (Netflix may or may not be on in the background)	**S2R**—Send to Receive (refers to sending nude pictures or videos)
9—Parent watching	**WTTP**—Want to trade pictures?
POS—Parent over shoulder	**420**—Marijuana

CHAPTER 3

Pandora's Box: School Issued Devices

A re our schools unknowingly giving out Pandora's Box, creating tech and porn addicts with school-issued tablets and laptops?

According to an article written by Cyrus Mistry,[13] group product manager of Chromebooks for Education at Google (who should know its own numbers), *"More than 25 million teachers and students are using Chromebooks for education globally and 30 million teachers and students are using Google Classroom, along with the 80 million using G Suite for Education."*

What is interesting about this article is that they say "globally," yet they have an interactive map with this article that shows the majority of the Chromebooks and Google Classroom are being used in the United States and Canada.

School-issued laptops and tablets are steadily replacing workbooks and textbooks. The kids love it! It is exciting: a shiny new device they get all to themselves, something that they do not have to share with siblings or parents. No more lugging a twenty-pound backpack full of "books."

Most parents think that schools issuing laptops and tablets is great news! Now they can cross off pencils, paper, notebooks, and other "archaic" items on the never-ending back-to-school shopping list.

No longer must you make sure your child has all his textbooks when he leaves each morning, prodding him to remember where he left his math book. Maybe at a friend's? Or did it fall behind the sofa? It also takes away the chance of mysteriously missing homework. Do dogs still eat homework? Chris Good, one of the authors of this book, says that his dog ate his homework several times.

While at first glance this all sounds great, many parents we encounter still have mixed feelings, even quietly questioning if it is a good idea to use computers for all subjects in the first place.

The devices themselves are harmless, and the intentions are good. Our kids need to learn technology to compete in today's workforce.

One of the dangers lurking is that many of the schools now require access to the internet to complete assignments. While on school property, the child's school-issued device is behind an internet filter to keep them from visiting inappropriate sites. It's when they leave school with their devices that problems can occur.

With Wi-Fi freely available just about anywhere your children go, they can easily have unrestricted access to the internet. All the places that your child can go and access the internet, including your home, may not have the same strict filtering policies as onsite at the school. Some school districts do have a filtering policy that follows the device no matter where it goes. You will need to check with your school directly to see if it is using this option.

Schools handing out devices will either send home or email device guidelines. This information will include rules for the device's use, including acceptable uses of the device and the consequences for misuse. In the business world, this is known as an Acceptable Use Policy, or AUP.

However, it is still up to you to figure out how this new device is used at home as well as monitor how your child uses the device.

You cannot rely on your child to self-monitor and follow the rules. I know we all want to believe that our children are the exception, but really, do you remember being twelve to sixteen years old and some of the crazy things your friends did? Enough said.

Another concerning area for some parents is the privacy problem. Believe it or not, there are some parents who say, "Privacy is dead in America; who cares what they collect."

To these parents we say, "I don't think you understand the impact the collection of that data can and will have on your child's future, including their college or professional future."

Whether you know it or not, there is a remarkable amount of personal information about children now being collected by schools and their vendors that is then shared with government agencies, for-profit companies, and other entities, all without parental consent.[14]

What kind of data? The personal data collected from children may include students' names, email addresses, grades, test scores, disability status and health records, suspension and discipline data, country of birth, family background, and more.

Other digital data collected may include internet search history, videos watched, survey questions, lunch items purchased, heart rate and other biometric information measured during gym class, and even classroom behavior, such as being off-task, nodding off, or speaking out of turn.

This information, whether collected by schools directly or by vendors supplying online learning platforms, classroom applications, and websites, is often merged together and analyzed via algorithms to profile a student's skills, strengths, abilities, and interests, and to predict future outcomes.

This information is taken and processed without taking into consideration that children change and mature, some faster than others. Some of the most brilliant minds in history went through a rough patch as a child. Henry Ford and Thomas Edison are just a few that come to mind. What would the collection of their data as children have said about them? Would it have affected their ability to have such an impact on the world and others around them?

Some schools offer an opt-out with alternatives to receiving a school-issued device. Some schools have instituted an "on premise only" policy, whereby the devices are kept and used only at the school. Other schools are leaving parents no choice, and if your child is attending the school, they must use the school-issued device.

Here are our top three questions you should ask about your kid's school-issued device:

1. How much time should my child be spending on the device each night? Now that laptops and tablets are mainstream in schools, schools and teachers should know approximately how much time it should take the average child to complete their homework or lessons.

Knowing approximately how much time and for what purpose

your child is using a device at home can help you better manage their overall screen time and make sure they aren't using their device to surf the web, watch YouTube videos, chat with friends, or engage in other online activities that aren't school-related. It will also help you ensure they are getting enough physical activity, face-to-face conversations, and fresh air.

2. Is there software on the device that tracks where my child goes on the internet? Is there software that is tracking how much time my child spends on the device? You may not know, but there was a lawsuit filed against a Pennsylvania school district that was monitoring and spying on students at home through the webcams. The school in question settled the lawsuits with the students that they had been monitoring without their consent through web cameras on school-issued laptops.

While we agree no one should be spying on your child through the device, tracking where a student goes online and how much time is spent on the device through software can serve as an early warning sign that something is wrong.

ALL educational applications on a school-issued device are tracking your child.[15] When your child is in school, whether on their issued device or a device that stays at school, where they go online, how long they visit that site, how long they are online, and sometimes where they clicked on the page are all being tracked.

Ask to see your school's data collection and privacy policy for school-issued devices if it was not provided with the Acceptable Use Policy when the device was issued.

Follow-up question: Ask if you can have a copy of your child's web history and usage report every month or quarter. If the answer is no, ask if anyone is checking these reports or if they just get logged and filed away. If you get the deer in the headlights look or there is nothing but crickets, you should follow up with your school board members.

In this age, these are serious questions that should have a concrete answer. Another tip: get the answer in writing. After you have asked the question and they have provided the answer, say, "Can you please email that over to me? Or can you direct me to the section of the school's website where I can find that in writing?" Even if they say they don't know the answer, get that in writing.

3. Are there parental controls or filters on the laptop that will work outside of the school's network? If not, can I install them? Ask if there is any type of documentation they can provide that lists the filtering standards that are being used on the device. For example: is only pornography blocked, or is the school also blocking chat rooms and social media sites?

In most schools when children use the school's Wi-Fi during the day, the network is filtered, meaning they cannot access inappropriate content such as pornography, information about drugs, social media sites, and games. But when they come home, unless you have filters on your home network, the gates to the internet are open.

Some schools have realized the dangers this poses to children and are using products that "follow" the devices anywhere they go, such as Sophos. This is great news for parents. However, this extra layer of protection comes at a cost. Not all school districts have the budget to add this layer of protection. Again, this is where you will need to be actively involved as a parent and ask your school about its policies.

School-issued devices are normally "locked down" by the school's IT staff, which means you cannot download or install any other software.

If you are not able to install anything on a school-issued device and the school's filtering does not follow the device wherever it goes, then you need to set up your own defenses at home.

If you are not an IT professional or have a strong IT background, we recommend that you reach out to a competent IT provider for assistance with this.

Just about all the internet service providers offer filters, as well as other features, either free or at an additional cost. Your kids are much smarter than you when it comes to technology and can bypass all the free and easy filters. We recommend having a more robust system that they are not able to bypass.

Some of our suggestions include Sophos, SonicWall, and OpenDNS. Any competent IT provider can set these up for you.

If there is one comment we hear repeatedly from parents about school-issued devices, it's this: "My child never gets off his device, and when I ask him to, he says he's doing homework. What can I do?"

This is a tough topic. The bottom line is, no matter what comes home from the school, *your* house equals *your* rules. That means you can still establish screen-free times such as family and dinnertime, as well as device-free zones, such as bedrooms. You can and should have rules about where devices are used, when devices get shut down at night, and where they're charged (outside of kids' bedrooms!).

If you think your child is doing more than homework on his device, then our suggestion is to grab a seat beside your child and say, "Hey, I just want to see what they are teaching you now in the twenty-first century, since I'm so old."

Make it light and funny, but sit with your kids. It may be uncomfortable, but who knows, you may end up having some of the best conversations that you've had since they were seven years old and didn't know that you weren't "cool."

What About YouTube?

Just about everyone has watched a YouTube video. From the really great "How to make a potato launcher" to those crazy dog and cat videos, YouTube videos are in abundance and children LOVE to watch them.

The majority of all devices being handed out in schools are the Google Chromebooks. These allow students to use the Google "G Suite" required for school. One of the downsides to the use of school Chromebooks is that you cannot turn off YouTube, and not all schools are filtering or blocking YouTube content.

I don't know about you, but there has been more than one occasion—well, it's almost every single time that I have watched a YouTube video—the next thing I know, something borderline inappropriate and sometimes obscene (resembling pornography) shows up on the right side of the screen as the next video that I should watch!

When our kids were little, we never watched a YouTube video when they were in the room, just for that reason.

There are over three hundred hours of video footage uploaded to YouTube every minute. Due to this insane volume, YouTube relies on algorithms to screen keywords, URLs, and content for inappropriate footage.

Unfortunately, math and morality just do not mix. When you factor in the sheer quantity of content uploaded, it makes it impossible for YouTube to hire enough staff to review even a small percentage of the videos that are uploaded.

YouTube is in the business of making money, and if that means your child sees Logan Paul[16] post a video standing beside someone who just committed suicide in Japan, well, that's not really their problem. They aren't in business to protect underage viewers.

Let us say, while we are business owners ourselves and have nothing against making a profit, we strongly disagree with any company that puts profit above **protecting children.**

Well, What About YouTube Kids?

In the fall of 2017, a group of mommy bloggers took aim at YouTube Kids due to an enormous number of inappropriate cartoon-like videos that snuck their way past YouTube's filters (see preceding comments related to algorithms trying to enforce morality).

You might remember hearing the phrase "Elsa Gate,"[17] since many of these videos included thumbnail images and descriptions that looked like innocent Disney princess videos, but were in reality a sick mix of adults in costumes and creepy cartoons with Disney-like characters doing weird and inappropriate things.

In all of the issues noted above, math, video quantity, and lack of human touch played a role in the situation.

Many good parents thought they were doing the right thing by allowing their children to use YouTube Kids instead of YouTube. How could Google let them down?

Here are two things to keep in mind:
1. Anything that says it is for kids on the internet still has a profit motivation. Maybe I'm overly cynical, but everything connected to the internet should be approached with a "verify before trust" mindset.

2. No app should be permitted to be used by kids until parents have completely vetted it. A good rule of thumb is the "seven-day rule." This means that no child in the family should use any app until you, the parent (or your spouse), have used it for seven days straight.

Look for the pop-up ads on day four compared to day one. What kind of language is used on level five that you did not see on level two? It should not matter what cartoon character is on the app or if Disney endorsed it!

Consider the revelation that sixty-three apps for kids that were listed for download on Google were displaying pornographic pop-up ads. Go seven days. Then ask yourself, "Is my son or daughter ready for everything that I just experienced?"

To make matters worse, Google halted the ability to create new supervised users on Chromebooks. Existing supervised users and the related settings were frozen, and the ability to see all visited URLs by existing supervised users was eliminated, making parental controls built into Chromebooks almost negligible.

The new product that replaced supervised users as of September 2018 is called Family Link. You will still need to check with your school and see if you can run this on its school-issued devices.

Parents Beware! We recommend that you read the privacy policies for Family Link yourself before using this with your family.

Here is just one of the alarming notices contained in the privacy policy:

When Your Child Can Manage Their Account on Their Own
When your child turns 13 (or the relevant age as determined by applicable law in your jurisdiction), they are eligible to manage their account on their own. If your child chooses to manage their Google Account, you will no longer have access to, or be able to exercise control over their account, unless you and your child later choose to set up supervision again through Family Link. Before your child becomes eligible to manage their own Google Account, we will notify you and your child.

According to Google, once your child is thirteen years old,

they can manage their account on their own, without you. Wow! How many thirteen-year-olds would you allow to manage their account on their own with no supervision?

There is more information in the privacy policy that is not good, like how they track your child and what they track. Google is essentially the NSA (National Security Agency) in the private sector.

What is a parent to do? The quick answer is to enable router-level filtering (or a good firewall) and have a monitoring service allowing you to review where the devices in your home are going on the internet.

While Google should take some responsibility in providing parental controls, ones that do not include tracking, storing, and selling all the data about our children, especially when they have a product that is geared for kids, we must remember that in the end, it is *our responsibility* as parents to monitor and be vigilant about what our children see.

Our last piece of advice when it comes to school-issued devices is to make sure you understand exactly what your kids can and cannot do with their school-issued devices as well as what happens if they break the rules.

You may be required to pay for the device. Also, depending on what your child does, it can also be reported to the police, land your child in trouble, and land you in jail.

In this new digital world, we as parents need to be more involved than ever, especially when it comes to school-issued devices. None of us must ever forget that the internet might have been created as a place to transfer academic information, but it has evolved into something different:

A place for the very best and very worst of humanity to **freely** share whatever they want.

What You Can Do:

- Make sure you and your children know the rules for the device and the consequences for breaking those rules.

- Have a "bedroom is off limits" policy. Keep devices in a central location for use, charging, and storage, like the kitchen, living room, or family room only.

- Periodically sit down with your children when they are doing their homework.

- Have a professional-grade firewall at home to filter and block your kids from going places they should not on the internet. Most times, the road to danger starts by *accidently* "finding" something.

- Monitor your internet traffic. Some professional-grade firewalls have the ability to monitor the internet traffic at your home and email you a daily, weekly, or monthly report of websites visited by what device, including any school-issued devices using your home internet service. *If you put one of these in place, please review the reports you receive.*

- Check to see if any of your neighbors have an unsecure Wi-Fi that your children can access. The easiest way to do this is to go to the Wi-Fi settings on your phone, tablet, or laptop. Anything

What You Can Do:

that shows up as "Open" means anyone can access the internet. Anything that shows up as "Secure" means that a password will be required to use the internet through that connection.

- Check to see if there are any in-range phone "hotspots" that your child can access. These will normally show up listed as "Person's phone name hotspot" under Wi-Fi settings. Click on the name and if you are automatically connected, that means your child can connect to that person's phone and use their Wi-Fi.

Note: If you find that unsecured networks are available, the best thing you can do is contact a reputable IT provider. We do not recommend you go knocking on each of your neighbors' doors to find out whose network it might be.

- Turn off the Wi-Fi hotspot option on your child's cell phone. You can do this by calling or visiting your cell phone carrier. Some providers have the option to block or turn off this feature/function in your online account.

CHAPTER 4

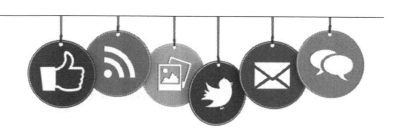

Smartphones: Are They Necessary and at What Age?

"Lisa, I have a question to ask and I know that you won't judge." Amber's voice cracked. I could tell she was on the verge of crying.

"I won't judge and I'll do my very best to help in whatever way I can."

"I noticed light in Lenny's room last night when I used the bathroom. When I opened his door, he tried to shove his phone under the covers." Now she was crying. "When I took his phone I couldn't believe it—he was watching a porn movie!" Now her sobs were uncontrollable.

"Amber, I'm so sorry."

"That's not the worst part. When Mike and I asked him what percentage of your friends do this, he said, 100 percent and that he learned how to connect to the neighbors' Wi-Fi from one of the older kids at school."

That call back in 2011 changed her life and mine. Her husband was an assistant pastor at a local church, who was forced to resign. They eventually moved back to Texas.

Would it surprise you to learn that both Bill Gates, founder of Microsoft, and Steve Jobs, founder of Apple, restricted their children's technology use and severely limited it in their homes?

Bill Gates did not let his children have cell phones until they were fourteen years old. Steve Jobs did not let his children use the iPad. Hard to imagine, isn't it?

I know what you are thinking: their kids didn't need to have a cell phone...

We understand the underpinnings of why you want your children to have a cell phone. We are well aware of the school shootings, kidnappings, and other incidents that parents have to contend with today.

According to the 2017 Nielson study,[18] 45 percent of kids get their first smartphone between the ages of eight and ten years old.

We also believe that as parents, you should know that giving your child a smartphone is like handing over the keys to a new car and a Platinum AMEX and saying, "Sweetheart, you can go wherever you want to go." It's a powerful device that can ruin lives, just like drugs and drunk driving.

Unfortunately, most parents have "NMK" ("not my kid") syndrome. If it can happen to an assistant pastor's child, it could happen to anyone.

We are not going to give a specific age that a child should have a phone. We believe the decision of when a child should be given a cell phone, especially a smartphone, should be based on maturity and circumstances.

Using our own children as an example, our oldest son didn't have a cell phone until he was sixteen years old, and he got Mom's old iPhone. (Moms and Dads, you should get the new phone, and the kids get the hand-me-down, unless the kids are paying for it.)

However, our youngest daughter got a cell phone at thirteen years old. Our decision around her phone had to do with her oldest siblings driving and we needed a way for all six of us to communicate. The phone she received was also a hand-me-down phone so she could make and receive calls—no internet and not a new top-of-the-line iPhone or Android.

Whenever Lisa is talking with a group of moms, it never fails: She is always asked about tech gadgets, internet safety, and what we personally do as parents, since we own a "tech" company.

She usually talks about what we do with our children, the real dangers kids today face, as well as how they as parents should be having meaningful and truthful conversations with their children about all of it, as uncomfortable as some of it may be.

There will always be at least one mom in the group who says, "That is exactly why I will never buy my child a cell phone. They can get one when they are eighteen."

To which Lisa responds, "Then you are setting your child up to go completely off the rails and either become a victim or an addict as soon as they can buy their own phone." Obviously, she does not win many popularity contests among the other moms.

Right now in the United States, 100 percent of people ages eighteen through twenty-nine own a cell phone, according to the Pew Research Center.[19] *One hundred percent.* Obviously, the children whose parents denied them a cell phone while living at home go out and buy one as soon as they turn eighteen.

While there are dangers that come with children having a cell phone, there are also benefits. I feel the majority of today's technology experts focus solely on all the possible dangers. As technology experts ourselves, we can understand the why behind this. However, we are parents, too.

For that reason, we are going to start by listing the benefits and positive reasons children should have a cell phone. You'll notice we didn't say "smartphone." A cell phone for a younger child can be a basic cell phone. They are sometimes referred to as a dumb phone, feature phone, or flip phone. They will work perfectly for younger children.

Convenience

How many times have you rushed from work to pick up your child from soccer only to get there and wait thirty minutes because practice started late? A phone allows your child to send a quick text letting you know they are running behind, so you do not waste your time.

Or think about when you are running late picking up your child from dance class or another after-school activity because of traffic. Instead of your daughter or son standing by themselves worried you have forgotten them, you can send them a quick message.

Another convenience is the tracking features that some, including parents, may call stalking, but I call old-school parenting. It is nice to be able to check with a few taps (and without nagging) to see if your child has made it to football practice or to a friend's house.

Safety

As unpleasant as it is to talk about, when you send your child off to school in the morning, you never know what type of emergencies your children may face. There could be a school bus accident, car accident, or a school shooter threat. Your child might also be feeling uncomfortable at a party when everyone starts drinking alcohol or trying a marijuana joint they found in their older sibling's room. A cell phone can be a lifesaver for a teen or tween to notify someone for help.

Side note: For older teenagers, the navigational tools are helpful if you have an older vehicle that does not have a built-in GPS. When kids start driving, teaching them how to use these (hands-free) can save them from a lot of stress and from getting lost.

Responsibility

Just like buying a dog can teach responsibility, a phone helps children learn how to do things for themselves. Older kids can use reminders for schoolwork or tasks for church or clubs. You can set up shared calendars for the family, where the children can also keep track of practices and work schedules. Gone are the days of day planners, except for us old-school holdouts! Most children have their phones with them all the time, unless you have house rules of when they can use them.

Remember, most kids want these phones and, if mature enough, will take care of them with some guidance. A side benefit we are told happens is they likely will not tire of them, like with a dog, and you won't get stuck with them when they head off to college. Ask us in a few years and we will tell you if this is accurate.

Connectivity

There is no doubt that children communicate mostly with their friends through phones. We cover the dangers of connectivity in another chapter. However, there is a positive: talking with family. Not texting, talking.

Our children call their "Great Granny" (who is eighty-seven years old) and chat with her several times during the week. They also talk with their Great Aunt Pearl and other family members who live states away. While our kids use the "house" phone to connect, most families today in America have gotten rid of their land lines and only have cell phones. We are one of the holdouts that still have a land line.

The ability of aunts, uncles, and extended family to keep up with and have real spoken conversations with your children is invaluable. It is something that texting and social media *cannot* teach or give them.

I believe this is a good list of benefits, or pros, if you will, of a child having a phone at a younger age. Now let's touch on some of the downsides, or dangers. We are going to keep these in the realm of not over-the-top extreme and scary. One of the challenges for us is to balance what we have seen (some of the things would make you unplug all the devices in your home and throw them in the trash) and what "most" people will *actually* encounter.

Poor Academics

It's very easy for children of all ages to become addicted to cell phones. Think about how many adults you know that cannot go through dinner or a social gathering without checking their phone. Cell phones allow children to play games, text, and talk to their friends.

For many students, their cell phones accompany them to school every day, just like their backpacks and school supplies. They talk on their phone in between classes and at lunch, as well as send text messages during class. They are not fully present and miss the lesson taught, often falling behind the other students.

Social Media Addiction

For most of us reading this, we grew up without phones. We really have no idea what it is like to go through the teenage years with social media. However, if you can remember that far back, imagine if you could see everything the guy or girl you liked was doing, all day long. You see whom they are dating, where they go, when they argue, and when they break up—in real time.

Can you imagine yourself as a teenager and having the self-control to monitor your use of your phone, tablet, or computer? If you are really honest with yourself, the answer is *no*. It is really a setup for failure.

Texting and Sexting

Then there is the epidemic of texting and sending inappropriate pictures, called sexting. Children as young as ten years old are sending nude photos.[20] More children have been mentally damaged from the images being passed around or posted on social media—not to mention the children who either attempt or commit suicide from the trauma, teasing, and bullying.

As of October 2018, twenty states have enacted sexting laws,[21] with others considering legislation. In states without specific sexting legislation, the possession of sexually explicit material portraying minors falls under the child pornography laws. This has the potential to result in felony charges and mandatory registration as a sex offender, even if your child is underage.

We cover sexting in a later chapter. The Parenting Technology Toolkit you receive when you register your book includes a resource of sexting laws by state.

Pornography

Children can also access pornographic sites from their cell phones. Yes, they can find this content on their computer or iPad, but with a smartphone, they literally have access to it all at their fingertips 24/7.

In December 2018, Pornhub, the internet's leading free pornography site, reported their 2018 statistics.[22]

Please do not go directly to this website—and if you google "2018 Pornhub statistics," be prepared for some frightening eye-opening information if you click the report link—this is NOT for the faint of heart! OK, you've been warned.

Traffic by Phone, Desktop & Tablet

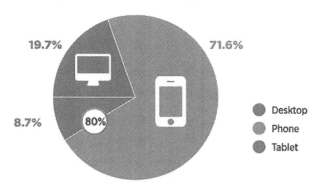

Change in Traffic Share from 2017 to 2018

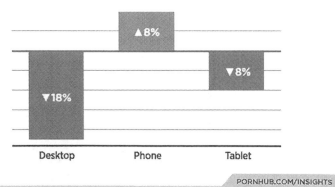

Here's a small sampling of statistics in relation to your children:

- 72 percent of pornography is viewed on smartphones.

- 9 percent of pornography is viewed via tablets.

- 62 percent of gaming console traffic comes from PlayStation.

- 33 percent of gaming console traffic comes from Xbox.

- More than half of online users ages eight and nine have encountered some form of pornography.

- 95 percent of online users ages ten through thirteen have encountered some form of pornography.

- One in five mobile searches is for pornography.

"Oh no," you might be thinking. *"Not my kid. He's not interested. She would never."*

Don't kid yourself. Your children may not be actively looking, but one search for an innocent term on an unprotected cell phone, tablet, or computer, and they can encounter something they or you didn't expect.

As one of our friend's sons told us, "I don't go looking for it intentionally, it finds me."

This is *not* the sex education most parents want for their children.

Development of Social Skills

Children today are spending less time socializing face-to-face. They can be in the same room and they will text each other before they will start a conversation. Face-to-face communication is one of the most important skills any human being can have. Their future life and work will be based on their ability to communicate.

Real communication and connection comes through verbal and facial cues. It is difficult to learn how to interact with humans and manage conflict appropriately if you are always behind a screen. Social skills are not something that can be learned through typing or texting.

Now that we have given you the *least* scary downsides, it really comes down to this: you have to decide what is right for your child. Once you make the commitment and buy them a phone, there is no turning back.

Make sure at the onset you guide them with boundaries (or rules for us old-school parents), parental controls including filtering software, lots of encouragement, and constant open communication. This *cannot* be a one-and-done deal.

For parents who have more than one child, I'm sure you already know this, but it's important to pay attention to how each of your children interacts with technology, specifically cell phones. The age at which one child gets a phone and their boundaries or rules can be completely different from those of your other children.

Who knew a phone could be such a monumental life-altering decision?

If you have not gotten your child a phone yet, but you are ready to take the plunge, check out the What You Can Do section at the end of this chapter for tips and suggestions before you put a phone in their hands.

What You Can Do:

You have decided your child is mature enough and ready to have their own phone. You've made the decision to go all in. You are going to get or give your child a smartphone (iPhone, Android).

Most of these tips would still be applicable even if you were getting your child a basic cell phone.

- Set clear guidelines both verbally and in writing before you go purchase or give your child their new phone. I know it sounds crazy—"in writing." Putting the guidelines in writing will make it seem like a very big deal for your child.

  We recommend making the guidelines have the look of a contract, where they sign and so do you. We know—you're the parents, and you shouldn't have to do that. You're right, you shouldn't.

  However, we have found that when you have things in writing on which everyone has agreed and understands, when infractions occur—and believe us, they will—you are no longer the bad guy when you impose whatever the agreed-upon consequences are.

  You went over them; your child agreed and has a copy of the

What You Can Do:

guidelines they signed. We know, you will still be the bad guy, but you'll be teaching your child the valuable lesson of breaking a written agreement.

- Establish that you are to know the password to the child's phone, and that you have the right to take it and look at it at any time.

We always say, "We have no intention of just grabbing your phone, but if we want to, we have every right to do so. We trust you, but we can and will verify that you are worthy of that trust."

- Set limits on both general screen time (games, music, videos) and phone time, including texting. This new device will whisper their name constantly. It's important to set up rules and limits at the very beginning.

- There are tools that have parental controls that allow you to setup screen time limits. Some of these tools will even shut your child's device off when they have reached their time limit.

- Specify when using the phone is not allowed, such as late at night or an hour before bedtime, when doing homework, and during family meals or family activities.

- Establish where the phone will "sleep" at night, which should not be in your child's room. There are inexpensive and great looking device holders that can be placed on the kitchen counter to charge and hold all devices overnight. Amazon.com is a great place to start your search.

- If your phone plan is not unlimited, make sure they understand and agree on when they can use their phone. Be very clear on this from the beginning or you could get an unexpected very big cell phone bill.

- List the consequences if they go over the phone plan limit. How will they pay for their phone usage? Lawn care, house cleaning, laundry, window washing…

- Implement a "text and phone are not to be used for important or emotional conversations" policy. Those must still take place face-to-face.

What You Can Do:

- Teach your child that the phone should not be used to hide or escape from uncomfortable situations and conversations.

- Be very clear about game and app purchases. This one can get you into some serious credit card debt. Apple does not care if your child racks up $5,000.00 in app purchases. You will be responsible for paying the bill. Many games promote themselves as "free," but then you have to buy weapons, or food for the animals or...to continue to the next level.

- We recommend that if your child has an iTunes account, you use a low-limit credit card and have the account set up to require you to approve every single purchase. Yes, it is a pain, but it would be much better than paying off a large credit card bill.

- Determine what the consequences will be if the phone is lost or broken. Will it be replaced? And, if so, who will pay for it? Again, we highly recommend you put this in writing. See your Parenting Technology Toolkit for a sample Parent–Child Cell Phone Agreement.

What You Can Do:

- If you allow your child to have social media accounts, have them give you all their passwords and add you to their "friends" list, and then monitor every site they use. Again, this is something that you should do from the beginning. While uncomfortable, you should also explain the "why" behind why you are doing this. This would also be a good time to explain that they shouldn't post anything they wouldn't be comfortable having their grandparents read.

- Consider using a GPS tracking tool on their phone. If your child ever comes up missing, this tool can be a valuable asset for the police or FBI.

- Ask questions that will spur conversations before giving them a phone, such as: What will you do when people are talking meanly about someone else in a group text? What will you do if someone tells a "secret" about someone else in a text? What will you do if someone sends a photo of themselves or someone you know that shows them without clothes?

- Put monitoring tools on their phone so that you know what they are downloading. There are many apps that you wouldn't want your kids to have access to, including certain dark web browsers.

What You Can Do:

We would like to cover two tips that would fall under the "My child already has a phone and NOW WHAT" category....

Let's tackle the most difficult one first.

- If your child is underage, in school, and living in your home, no matter what, you are their parent, and if they are completely out of control and doing inappropriate things with their phone or you believe they are going to harm themselves, please, take their phone and get them help immediately. You are their parent—not their friend—and you can and should step in.

- Your kids won't put down their phones. Have a family meeting and let them know that starting on XXX date, every day at dinner (or whenever you specify) everyone will turn off their phones and spend time together. However, you should expect grumbling, and some attempts to evade giving up their phones. You should continue on and model the manners and behaviors you want to see. Dr. Nido Qubein, president of High Point University, has said for years, "More is caught, than taught. Don't expect kids to follow the rules when they see you always breaking them."

CHAPTER 5

Smartphone Apps: Doorway to Danger and Hidden Secrets

P aula picked up her thirteen-year-old son's phone that sat on the kitchen counter. She typed in his password and swiped through the screens. Everything looked normal, iTunes, Kindle, Fandango, and FaceTime were just a few of the apps on his phone. He had a few game apps. She smiled when she saw the Tic-Tac-Toe app.

Interested to see how the digital version of Tic-Tac-Toe would play out, she clicked the app, only to be asked to input a password. Very strange, she thought. Paula would have never imagined that her world would be forever changed in that moment.

When she reached her son's room and demanded the password, what she saw shocked her. There were photos of Ryan half-naked and fully naked. There were also photos of various girls in the same condition. How could this be? It was supposed to be a Tic-Tac-Toe game!

Paula has just been introduced to the world of "vault" or secret apps.

Once your child has a smartphone and it becomes part of their daily life, they naturally learn about apps (applications) and all the fun and useful things that apps can do. Finding apps and trying out new apps on their phones is second nature to them.

Today's kids spend 81 percent of their time texting, followed by app use at 59 percent, which is cause for concern since 42 percent of apps do not encrypt the data they send to third parties.[23] Social apps like Facebook, Facebook Messenger, Instagram, and Snapchat are the leading apps being used. Children today live and interact through apps.

It is also common for kids to have secret apps, also known as vault or ghost apps, hiding in plain sight. Many of these vault apps listed for download on the Apple App Store are listed as safe for ages 4+.

In the "olden days" (read: our youth), we kept our most personal secrets with the whisper of a pen, safeguarded by a built-in miniature padlock, standard issue for private paper diaries. But let's be honest: those locks were easily circumvented, often with a paperclip or a bobby pin, should parents (or nosy siblings) have a gut feeling that there was something "juicy" hidden inside.

Now that we are in the digital age, our children's phones are their private diaries, and vault apps hide their secrets (photos, emails, phone calls, text messages) from prying eyes.

Some of the apps themselves are not inherently dangerous, while others are designed to hide things and specifically let teens do things that their parents would not approve of privately.

The best old-school example would be when you wanted to go to a party that you knew your parents wouldn't approve, and so did your friends. Therefore, you all conspired to tell your parents you were at the library, a school function, a certain friend's house, or a concert so that you could sneak out and go to the party. The problem with these apps is they are not just about going to a party you are not allowed to attend. These apps open up a world of danger for children, including kidnapping, drug use and overdose, pornography, meetings with strangers, and other serious situations.

So now you are likely wondering, "How would I know if my kids have any hidden apps and how would I find them?" That is a great question! If you do not already use a tool that alerts you to activity on your kid's mobile device, or you have teenagers, you will need to go with your gut on this, as well as be prepared to have a possibly uncomfortable conversation and demand to see their phone.

Here are some tell-tale signs that your child has hidden or ghost apps:

- Turning their device off or moving it away from your sight when they see you enter the room or come close to them.

- They are reluctant to hand over their phone for you to take a look.

- Shaking their phone or quickly flipping it over when you come into the room. Either one of these actions could mean they are using the "emergency close" feature of a vault app, otherwise known as the *nosy parent* close.

- A refusal to give you their passwords. If your child refuses to give you their password, there is a 99.9% chance they have something they are hiding and don't want you to see.

- If your child does hand their phone over, and you see duplicate apps on the phone, such as several calculator apps or photo apps, that's normally a sign that they are using a phony vault app to hide items they don't want you to see.

Vault apps will often look like other, common mobile device apps. The objective here is to blend in and seem like they are normal. You won't see an app called "naked photos" listed. The apps are made to hide in plain sight and look like apps your child would actually use. Some of the hidden apps we have seen look like texting, music, or book apps.

Think of the most unassuming app on your phone, one that you may or may not use a lot, and definitely not one that typically wouldn't raise a red flag if you're checking your child's device.

As parents, teachers, and the media discover and publicize the current vault and dangerous apps that kids are using, new apps take their place or the same app changes names, so it's almost impossible to provide a list of all the current dangerous apps your kids could be using in this book. A month after publication, any list provided here would be irrelevant.

Instead, we have listed the top three categories of apps—Hidden, Dating, and Video & Chat—then listed the most-used apps that have not changed. If you see any of these apps on your child's devices, they should raise a red flag and be cause for concern. See your Parenting Technology Toolkit for a more detailed list of vault apps.

1. Hidden or Vault Apps: Hidden or Vault apps your child may be using so that you don't know what they're up to are Vault, CoverMe, and Keep Safe. There are hundreds of other privacy apps: we've listed just a few. These apps allow a person (your children) to hide messages, pictures, and so on, but show up as an innocuous icon, such as a calculator or clock, when someone else logs into the phone. Some of these apps offer a security feature that takes your picture if you enter the wrong password, letting the phone's owner know who tried to access their app.

2. Dating or "Hook-Up" Apps: Flirting, dating, and, yes, even "hooking up" are a lot easier to do in the digital age. Today, downloading a dating app takes no more than a moment, and suddenly you have a whole world of possible "dates" at your fingertips. Most apps do not have any type of age verification process in place, which makes them dangerous for young children (even teenagers).

A few of the more popular choices are: Skout, MeetMe, and Down.

A word about Down. This app works through Facebook and its official description is "The secret way to get down with people nearby." In case you skipped "The Lingo of Today's Digital Kids" section, this **does not** mean hanging out or dancing.

When the app first came out in 2013, its description was "Bang with friends." I am sure you can figure that one out. While the app says it is for 17+, there is no age verification process, which allows any of today's tech-savvy kids to install it. As of January 2018, this app has more than five million users. Is your kid one of those users?

Online there are three in-depth review articles about this app. Two were written by Fast Company[24] and the other written by Android Apps For Me.[25] *Note: If you are brave enough to read these reviews, please do so **without** your children around.*

3. Video and Chat Apps: There are so many video and chat apps that it is impossible to keep up! Here are just a few apps that have been known to be more on the dangerous side: Ask.fm, Kik, and Omegle. See your Parenting Technology Toolkit for a more detailed list of video and chat apps.

A word about three of the most popular chat apps that children are using: Ask.fm, Kik, and Omegle. Ask.fm is a Q&A site where users can ask other users questions anonymously. The problem is that kids sometimes target one person and the questions get nasty. It is cyberbullying with no chance of ever getting caught. Ask.fm has been associated with nine documented cases of suicide.[26]

Kik Messenger is used by children for sexting and to place classified ads for sex on Reddit and other online forums. The Kik user policy states that children under the age of thirteen are not to use their app; therefore, there are no parental controls and no age verification. This is also one of the primary apps used by sexual predators[27] to interact with minors, including sexting unsolicited sexts.

Omegle is an online chat forum in which strangers are picked at random to chat. There is also an option that allows you to add your interests, after which you are paired with a stranger based on similar interests and can chat via messages and video. You do not need to register to use this service. Due to predator arrests and media attention, Omegle has added the following text to their site for liability: ***"Predators have been known to use Omegle, so please be careful."***[28]

The typical chat starts with "ASL," which means: Age? Sex? Location? When Omegle was first launched, the only way to use the service was through the app. After receiving negative media attention and thousands of parents removing the app from their children's phones, Omegle has revised its product. At the time of this writing, your child or anyone can use the service by just opening a web browser on their smartphone, tablet, laptop, or desktop and going directly to their website. No downloading or special "app" is required.

While we did not include Snapchat as a "red flag" app, you should still be careful about allowing your children to use it. According to Statista, as of April 2018, 63 percent of thirteen- and fourteen-year-olds and 74 percent of fifteen- through seventeen-year-olds in the United States use Snapchat as their primary chatting application.[29]

Many children feel comfortable sending inappropriate or sexually explicit photos or videos on Snapchat since they get to determine how long the receiver can see the image or video until it self-destructs.

Snapchat makes kids think their Snaps disappear forever, and ***they are wrong***. It is actually pretty easy for the receiver to recover a self-destructed Snap, take a screenshot of it, and share it with others. When we say "others," we mean forward via text message or post it on other social media platforms or porn sites.

What your child probably does not know is that many images from Snapchat are regularly posted to revenge porn sites, called "Snap porn." No parent wants to learn that a photo or video of their child is on a site like Snapperparty or Sexting Forum.

Just Google those names if you would like to search those sites to see if your child has any videos or photos posted. We have excluded the links for them in this book intentionally. Be warned: if you Google those sites, it will return a list of sites with disturbing language and images. *You absolutely should **not** do this on a computer your child has access to or uses.*

Snapchat has also launched Snap Map, which allows users to share their exact location with friends. If your children are using Snapchat, it is important to turn this feature off right away so other users cannot track them.

If you want to make sure your children cannot download ANY apps without your approval, here is a way to do that without monitoring software (although we highly recommend monitoring software, especially for younger children).

iPhones: Go to SETTINGS, GENERAL, RESTRICTIONS.

You will be prompted to create a code, and then you can select any phone functions to which you do not want your child to have free access without your permission.

Androids: You can set up parental controls via the Google Play store. Create a PIN that your kids do not know about, and put in filters for apps, games, and movies by choosing the maturity level of the content you want to allow.

You can also require a password for authentication for purchases in Google Play. Your child would need your Google password to change these settings, so make sure it's one they do not know. Additionally, you can set up a family payment method, where you can turn on purchase approval settings for family members.

While we do not personally use this tip, a government cybersecurity speaker suggests parents use a "four letter" word as their passcode. It's something few kids would EVER suspect and it will certainly be easy for you to remember.

As we close this chapter, we would like to emphasize that not all apps are bad or dangerous. There are hundreds of great apps your children can have, from the NASA app to apps that teach math, like the DragonBox Algebra app. It is important to have open communication with your child about what is appropriate to say or send in an app and have clear guidelines and rules about the use of their devices.

What You Can Do:

- Sit down and have an honest conversation with your children. Tell them that you know these apps exist and give them the opportunity to come clean if they have them before you take their phone and start searching for them.

  Although it is your right as a parent to just start searching, you won't be building trust with your child if you do. This is important if you have never had any discussions about appropriate use and/or you haven't set any rules about device use.

- Check their phone for duplicate apps, such as two calculators, chat apps, photo apps or special utility apps.

- Check their phone for hidden or vault apps. Go to the Google Play or Apple Store on your child's phone and do a couple of searches, such as "hidden apps" or "vault apps" or even "hide photos." If the word "GET" appears next to the app for download, that means the app is not on their phone. If the app is already on the phone, the word "OPEN" or "INSTALLED" appears next to the app. More often than not, this means that your child already has items hiding on their phone.

What You Can Do:

- If your children have iPhones, add them to your iCloud account. That way whenever a new app is downloaded, it will automatically download to your phone as well.

- You can install monitoring software on your child's phone. There are many different options on the market and they all have different features. See your Parenting Technology Toolkit for a more detailed list of monitoring software.

CHAPTER 6

Sexting: The Real Consequences

Donnie and Heather are typical parents. They have two children, a sixteen-year-old son and a thirteen-year-old daughter. Donnie is a truck driver and Heather is a nurse. One evening Heather takes the last few months of the cell phone bills to Donnie.

"I don't understand. Who could she be sending THAT many messages to?"

Donnie sighs, "She is a teenager, maybe it's a new friend. I'll go ask her."

Donnie asks Barbara, his daughter, who she is messaging so much, and she confesses that she is in love with a senior boy at a different school in their town. When Donnie takes her phone and starts looking at her messages, horror sets in.

She has been sending nude and partially nude photos to "John" but there aren't any photos from "John" on her phone. Donnie not only takes her phone, but he also reports the issue to the police and the police put a trace on "John's" phone number.

What came back scared them to the core. The phone number actually belonged to a fourteen-year-old girl at the other school, not a seventeen-year-old boy. The girl was catfishing (pretending to be someone you are not) other girls at the rival school and sending all the pictures she collected to everyone at her school.

While the school expelled the young girl, the damage done to Donnie's daughter and several other girls had already been done, and it could never be reversed.

So much has changed since most of us were kids—you know way back in the 1900s. When I was fourteen years old (this is Lisa speaking here), I talked on the phone a lot. So much so that my mom instituted time limits per call and per friend! There were long chats with my girlfriends and awkward chats with boys (which my dad listened in on secretly).

I'd have to dial the wall-mounted beige rotary phone in my kitchen and then have a polite conversation with my friend's mom or dad before the phone was passed to my pal so we could chat about school, the weekend, and friend drama.

Back then, if a girl wanted to show a boy her body (or vice versa), they would have to be somewhere semi-private; evade parents, siblings, or other adults that may be in the house or the vicinity and only then take off their clothes.

For children today, all it takes is their cell phone in hand, locking the door in their room or bathroom, and a few clicks. It is that easy, it is an epidemic with kids today, and if you think "not my kids," you are most likely fooling yourself.

If we as parents do not address the current issues in our children's lives, including the issues we don't know much about and didn't have to deal with when we were their age, they will get this information elsewhere. They will turn to their peers or older siblings, neither of which are generally the best sources when it comes to giving wise advice. The problem is it often leaves our kids misinformed.

Sometimes one "foolish" iPhone photo can derail your child's entire life.

If you were to ask your local law enforcement agencies (police or sheriff) or school counselors, they can tell you how truly rampant this behavior is. What was once a random act is now the norm; they see it every day.

Some parents believe that if they have their child in a private school or even home schooled, they are not participating in this behavior. However, that is a myth. Sexting has gained a presence with children from every demographic—rich and poor, urban and rural, no matter your race or religion.

There are two main schools of thought from the professionals (psychologists, doctors, etc.) when it comes to dealing with sexting. The first is: it's not that big of a deal; this is just the emerging and potentially new normal part of modern-day sexual behavior and development, so parents should not be too concerned.

The second is: it's a predictor of sexual behavior and may be associated with other risky behaviors, such as bullying, drug use, and suicide, and is a guarantee to ruin their future.

If the so-called "experts" cannot agree on the topic, what is a parent to do?

We have talked in previous chapters about using monitoring software on your child's cell phone. While we believe monitoring software is a valuable tool for parents, we would like to give a warning.

The "spy" type of monitoring software that secretly logs and watches everything a child does can easily backfire. You have to remember that your primary goal as a parent is to teach your children how to make sound decisions and guide them to independence. No amount of monitoring software is going to replace talking with and having a relationship with your child.

As parents ourselves and as parents who are deep into the tech sector, especially security, here is our advice. Talk with your children and start early. Don't have one conversation on the day that you give them their first cell phone and think you're done. Talk to them often—have many different conversations over their childhood and into adulthood.

Parents, please do not assume that only girls are sexting, boys are just as likely. So make sure you have the sexting talk with both your boys and girls.

Photos that boys send are more likely to be forwarded. Just like girls' gossip, forwarding a boy's photos is the ultimate form of gossip today.

We know that these conversations will be uncomfortable and not feel normal, but you should have them nonetheless. For younger children, the conversations could be simple and put in the context of other absolute rules.

For example, when you are teaching and talking about not getting into a car with a stranger, you can also add that text messages, emails, and online chats should never include anyone with no clothes.

As those conversations progress, they should include the "what if" scenarios: What if you feel pressured to send an inappropriate text (partially clothed or nude photo) and you don't want to? What do you think you should do? Who would you talk to? Who should you talk to?

As children get older, especially middle and high school ages, conversations can and should become more direct. Most parents' conversation about sexting consists of "Do NOT send nude photos!" End of conversation. We also need to remind our children that they should not ask anyone to send them nude photos either.

Most research conducted about who is sexting more, boys or girls, has found little difference.[30] However, not surprisingly, research shows that boys are four times more likely to pressure girls to send sexts than vice versa, meaning girls feel more pressure to sext and girls worry more about the consequences of sexting such as slut shaming for sexting or, alternatively, being called a prude for not sexting.

You could even play the "what would you do" game. This consists of giving believable real-world examples to your child and asking, "What would you do if that happened to you?" If you are having trouble coming up with believable examples, we have developed a fifty-question guide based on real-world scenarios that can assist with this topic.

While this all sounds like foolish romantic things teenagers do, there are real dangers as well as serious and sometimes deadly consequences of sexting. Here are the top five.

1. Sexting can lead to bullying. Once a photo is sent, your child loses all control over the image. People can use it in any way they want. Unfortunately, many people will use the images to sexually bully the person in the photo.

One example of sexual bullying is called slut shaming. In these instances, people make assumptions about the child's willingness to engage in sexual activity. They also may make assumptions about the child's reputation. Meanwhile, the receiver of the photo might share the photo online to embarrass and humiliate the boy or girl in the photo.

The photo or photos may also be used to impersonate the person in the picture and post inappropriate comments and remarks. There are documented cases of young adults committing suicide due to bullying over photos that they sent and that had been shared.

2. Sexting can lead to blackmail. Sometimes when a child sends a nude photo during an impulsive moment, they are later at risk for being blackmailed. There have been cases where the recipient of the image threatened to publicly shame the sender unless they complied with the blackmailer's demands.[31]

Many children who are subjected to these types of threats give in. They are often too embarrassed to ask anyone for help and may be at the mercy of the blackmailer for a long time.

Just as there are documented cases of young adults committing suicide due to bullying about photos that they shared, there are also documented cases of suicide due to not being able to take any more blackmail. The perceived shame drove these young adults to take their own lives.

3. Sexting can lead to jail time, felony charges, and having their name registered on the sex offenders' list—because sexting constitutes child pornography. When nude pictures or partially nude pictures involve minors, this is considered child pornography in many states. While state laws vary about the rules and regulations of sexting, in some states, exchanging nude photos of minors is considered a felony, even when the photos being taken and shared are consensual.

For instance, the teen taking or sharing the photo can be charged with disseminating child pornography. Meanwhile, the person receiving the photo can be charged with possession of child pornography, even if the person *did not request that the photo be sent*.

What's more, teens can be labeled sex offenders for sending or possessing sexually explicit photos of other teens. There have even been cases where teens were charged with a crime, even though the photos were of them.

Yet as many as 61 percent of teens do not realize that sexting could be considered child pornography.[32] Nearly as many said that if they had known, it "probably would have" deterred them from sexting, which is why it is so important to have conversations with your children and not just say, "Don't do it."

4. Sexting can open the door to sexual predators. Although the photo is usually intended for only one person's eyes, there is no way to control who sees the photo once your child sends it.

In fact, there are countless cases where a child sent a sexually provocative photo and then later found that this photo was on various pornography and pedophilic websites. Sometimes the receiver uploads the photo to these websites. This behavior actually has a name: revenge porn.

In other instances, the photos are stolen from social media sites and uploaded without either party's knowledge. When this happens, your child is at an increased risk of being blackmailed or sexually exploited by people who claim to be someone they are not.

5. Sexting can (and often does) cause shame and destroy future opportunities. Once photos are in the digital realm, they NEVER go away. Ever. If they made it onto Facebook, thirty years from now, someone will be able to search and find those photos.

Many kids mistakenly believe that a photo sent via Snapchat (or any other app that automatically deletes messages after they are viewed) will only be able to be viewed by the recipient. They believe the images they just sent are being deleted automatically in a matter of seconds, but kids have learned how to copy images and save them before the app deletes them.

Nude photos and other photos showing risky behavior online can haunt a college applicant or job seeker years later. Many colleges and employers check online profiles, looking for signs of a candidate's maturity or giant red flags about bad judgment.

Some states have passed laws trying to prevent employers from discriminating against applicants based on their social media accounts and to prevent employers from asking applicants to show them their social media accounts. Even in those states, companies have found ways to go around those laws, and they are checking every applicant.

If your son or daughter has anything that appears to offend, does not fit into the "culture," or shows a lack of judgment, your child receives a polite and reasonable rejection call or letter. Your son or daughter will never know the "real reason" they were not accepted to that school, did not get the new job, or were passed over for promotion.

Be sure your child knows these risks as early as possible.

Again, we know this is uncomfortable. It is just like talking about sex with your child—because in a way, it is sex. It is worth talking about.

According to an article in the American Medical Association Journal, *JAMA Pediatrics*, "Kids who report discussing sexting with their parents are less likely to sext and less likely to have a traumatic outcome if they do sext."[33]

And to that point, parents, try to keep yourself in check if or when things go wrong. Obviously, no one wants their child to sext, just like most parents don't want their teenagers to get pregnant. The difference here is that sexting is so prevalent that the odds of you dealing with it at some point are high. How you deal with it, if and when it occurs, can either build or break your relationship with your child.

If things have gone wrong, it may help to think about the risky things you did (be honest) when you were younger before you have a discussion with your child.

For those of us that have not grown up in this digital era, it sounds crazy: WHY would you want to send THAT?!? Try to view sexting through their lens: here is something today that most of their friends and people around them are doing, so it feels like a normal thing to do and a normal thing to ask. They are living in the moment and not considering the danger or lasting consequences.

What You Can Do:

- Teach and encourage your child/teen to ask themselves the following questions about what they are sharing:

  1. Is this how I want people to see me?
  2. Could somebody use this to hurt me?
  3. Would I be upset if they shared it with others?
  4. What is the worst thing that could happen if I shared this?

- Discuss appropriate ways of showing you care for someone. When someone really cares about you, they will not pressure you into doing anything that you don't want to do.

- Remind your child frequently to ask themselves the questions above before sharing something personal, especially provocative photos.

- Remind your child they should not do anything they do not want to. Tell your child that if somebody asks them to send something they are not comfortable doing, they have the right to say no.

- Talk about respect and ethical decision making. Teach your children the "do not pass it on" rule if they have been forwarded someone else's photos.

What You Can Do:

- Remind your child to always ask themselves how they would feel if someone forwarded their photo to friends at school.

- Let your child know that while their friend who sent the photo may have meant it as a joke, anything that would embarrass or hurt someone else is not a joke.

    Most kids who forward sexts do not think of it as being wrong (crazy, we know). It goes back to the way our children see famous people living their lives and making their fortunes on social media.

- Teach and encourage your child/teen to ask themselves the following questions when someone shares a sext with them: 1. Did the person in this picture mean for it to be shared? 2. If it came from someone other than the original sender, did they have permission from the person who's in it? (Most likely not.) 3. How would I feel if somebody shared something like this with me in it?

- Encourage your kids (today) to delete any inappropriate photos they may have on their phone.

What You Can Do:

- Remind your child *repeatedly* that once an image is in the world, you *cannot* take it back. It is possible that the image could eventually reach unintended audiences: extended family (grandparents, aunts, uncles, cousins), teachers, future employers, kids they babysit, etc.

- Check your school's policy and your state's laws on sexting. While you as a parent may not dissuade them from sexting, they should know the potential implications of doing so.

- Make sure you are honest about the consequences from the school and the law if they send nude photos. It will not help you to make up or exaggerate the consequences to scare your child. Most kids know how to Google—often better than you.

- While this will be a controversial or "gray" area to some parents, we would also encourage you to discuss with your child under what circumstances they should come and talk to you if they have been forwarded someone else's photos or know that others are passing around another child's photos. You could be the one that may save another parent's child from danger or suicide.

- Most importantly, don't have one conversation—have many.

CHAPTER 7

Sharenting: Are YOU Endangering Your Children?

Are those cute baby photos you shared on social media of Junior getting his first bath also posted on a child pornography website?

Are those photos of your little princess romping around the kiddie pool in the backyard being used to find the next beauty to kidnap and either hold hostage or auction off as a sex slave?

It may sound a bit over the top, we know, but it happens more often than you think.

If you are a younger parent who has grown up in the "digital world" or an older parent who has embraced the "post it all on my blog or social media" craze, sharing photos and videos of your family online is probably part of your everyday life.

What many parents today do not realize is that "sharenting"—sharing pictures of your little ones (and older children) online—is overexposing them and could make them vulnerable to pedophiles, predators, kidnappers, and identity thieves.

It is estimated that today, by two years old, 90 percent of children in the United States have been featured on social media like Facebook, Instagram, Twitter, and Snapchat.[34]

As pure as your intentions may be in posting pictures and videos of your children sitting in a high chair naked while eating their first piece of birthday cake or splashing in the bath, you need to understand that there are predators online who seek to take advantage of that information and media.

We are going to be real here and realize that some of you will disagree with this. Personally we do not think you should post photos of your children bathing or any other photo that shows your child naked or even partly undressed.

Be honest: would you want some of the photos your parents took of you posted online, where they will be FOREVER? Where college professors, employers, fellow employees, and neighbors could find them? Nope, we would not have wanted that either. Let Aunt Elda see the photos when she comes to visit or show them to her when you go to visit.

Child predators routinely troll blogs, especially those "mommy" blogs and social media sites, seeking child pornography posted by unsuspecting and well-intentioned parents.

The thought of someone taking photos of children and using them in such a manner creates a fierce rage in us and in most parents we know. Statistics show that 85 percent of those who obtain and possess child pornography are also hands-on child abusers.[35]

Nearly 90 percent of parents who share photos of their children on social media platforms have not checked their privacy settings over the last year. Are you one of them? If you are, next time you open these apps, spend a few minutes going through your settings.

We believe it is great that most social media sites provide privacy setting options. You should definitely have them set up. Unfortunately, those options give you a false sense of security by promoting "private or protected" groups and settings. Just because you post to a private Facebook group you created or a protected Instagram account you set up, it does not mean your photos and videos are safe.

One of our local Drama Club moms is always posting photos of her kids and the theater. The problem with this is most of the pictures include other children that are not hers. Not everyone wants their children's lives posted online.

Remember, you as the parent have the right to dictate what is and is not shared online about your children. Please extend that courtesy to other parents whose children may be in your photos before you post them online.

We personally told all of our relatives and friends that we did not want ANY photos or videos of our children posted on any type of social media. We are the rarity, not the norm. In most cases, other parents will not mind and will appreciate being asked before you post.

If you are going to participate in digital sharing of your young children, you should balance your desire to share with the need to protect your children.

Unlike celebrities who need social media to capitalize on every detail of their lives to build their wealth, including everything their children do, you most likely do not have a security detail and bodyguards following you or your children to keep them safe.

You should also keep in mind that the data you are sharing is being stored and will be used by Google, other search algorithms, schools, the government, and future employers (either for or against your children) for years to come. Read: **FOREVER.**

What You Can Do:

- Check your social media settings. While privacy settings are not fail-proof, they are still important. We recommend that you check your settings at least every thirty days. Many of the sites release updates and new features. Not every time, but many times after a significant update is released, it will affect how your settings are used by third-party applications, friends, and even the company itself. If you have not checked your privacy settings in the last month, **you should do it right now**.

- Before you post something, ask yourself the following questions and when in doubt—leave it out:

  1. Is this photo embarrassing to my child?

  2. Could it cause him embarrassment in the future?

  3. Is this photo compromising in any way?

  4. Could it be viewed or used as sexual bait by a child predator or pedophile?

  5. Does it share too much information or infringe on anyone's privacy?

  6. Do I have permission from the other parents to post this photo with their child/children in it?

What You Can Do:

- Don't use hashtags for your children's photos. Those who are seeking or peddling child pornography look for certain hashtags to find photos, including #kidsbathing, #babybathtime, and #pottytraining. If you really love hashtags and cannot refrain, at least use them #sparingly and #thoughtfully.

- You should never use geotags on photos of your children. Sharing your child's location, like the school or the playground you frequent, provides a map for predators. There are children kidnapped every day! Please do not provide easy access to yours.

- Ask before you share. Whether you are the grandparent, aunt, or best friend, ask the parents of the children in your photos if it is OK to post and then tell them where you are going to post. Some parents may not mind, but others may ask you to not share.

- Think about your child's future. Everything you post will be cataloged somewhere forever. Nothing that is put on the internet is ever permanently deleted, and the right people with the right tools can find it.

Bill Gates, Steve Jobs, Warren Buffett, the Google founders, and just about all other affluent people do not have their "real" lives,

What You Can Do:

or their children's, on Facebook, Instagram, or any other social media site.

While most of them do have social media accounts, like Mark Zuckerberg, Bill Gates, etc., the dirty little secret is that they have a publicist that posts everything for them.

Every post you see is done strategically to advance their cause, their business, their brand—even those that look like heartfelt open letters.

Some of them, like Mark Zuckerberg, have a full-time photographer whose job it is to follow him around and get the "candid" photos you see posted online.

They know that everything is online forever. They do not want to be the cause of future damage to their children. ***Don't your children deserve the same advantage and consideration?***

Note: We are not talking about celebrities that make their living off of living life publicly and publicity stunts. They know as they age, they will need their children to be just like them to continue living large.

CHAPTER 8

A Social Reputation: It Will NEVER Go Away

James was a baseball player in high school. Kim was on the soccer team and wanted James to take her to homecoming. The problem was that James wasn't interested in Kim.

Instead of just leaving the answer to the verbal, "No, I don't want to go with you" he had already given her, on a Wednesday night he took to Twitter and tweeted, "Kim has slept w/ many friends on the team, now she wants me – um NO."

James was kicked off the baseball team, lost his baseball scholarship to college, was not permitted to attend homecoming, and was suspended from school for three days. Whether what he said was true or not, it should have never been "tweeted" out into the universe—a difficult life lesson that James just learned.

Most children think only their friends are reading what they post on social media. Even if their parents have access, most kids would tell you that their parents rarely look at their accounts; they are too busy with work and life. While there may be some truth in that, there is always someone watching, like teachers, coaches, bosses, and other parents. In James' case, his coach, the principal, and Kim's mom all saw his tweet.

In the pre-social media days when most of us were growing up, if you made a mistake, unless the offense was criminal, those incidents were quickly forgotten and did not follow you into adulthood.

For the sake of clarity, I am talking about nonviolent childish pranks, like toilet papering the grumpy old neighbor's trees and bushes or blocking their car door with a giant snowball in winter. Or maybe you had a brief stint of running with the "rough" crowd one year in high school, but you gave that up, learned some lessons, and are a better person for it.

Had social media been around for any of those events in your life, they could and would haunt you today. They could have a determining factor on where you could go to college, who you could marry, what type of work you did, or whether you got the promotion at work. They could even play a role in whether you could join the military or work in any branch of the government.

Unfair, you say! We agree. However, it does not change the

facts. That is precisely the world our children live in. As a parent, you really have three basic choices when it comes to social media and your children.

1. You can let your children loose in the new social world with no guidance, no rules, and no training. Unfortunately, this is the choice the majority of parents make.

2. You can teach, train, limit, assist, and monitor your children's participation in the social world. If you are going to let your kids participate, this choice will no doubt be challenging, but is much safer than choice number one.

3. You can keep your children out of the social world and encourage them to sit out until they are adults. After all, it is your house, your rules—right. This is the choice that Bill Gates, Steve Jobs, Warren Buffett, Mark Zuckerberg, the Google founders, and just about all affluent and tech industry people take *with their kids*. This choice is not easy. It requires courage and going against popular beliefs.

Now that we've covered the three basic choices, we are going to give some tips on choice number two.

If anyone is interested in how to do choice number three, please contact us offline. It would take entirely too long to give you the detailed plan to follow, and it would venture into the territory of parenting advice. We will say this is the road that we have our children on, but we are trying to keep this book about technology.

Here are the basics to teach your children about social media:

- **Nothing is ever really private.** Posts and pictures can be shared and altered, even with the most restrictive privacy settings in place. While sharing can be bad, altered can be worse.

- **Nothing is ever permanently deleted.** Everything is traceable. Even when someone deletes a post, comment, or picture, it exists somewhere online. Whether someone took a screenshot or it's just sitting in the archives, it is out there and others can find it. In addition, anyone who has seen or read it will remember; it definitely will not be forgotten.

- **Some things are better said face-to-face, like apologies or confrontations.** Social media makes it easier for people to be cowardly, or braver than they should be. Kids should be taught the value of looking someone in the eye and making things right. Sure, it is harder, but they will not forget it.

- **Remember there are real people with real feelings behind every avatar.** A keyboard and monitor are easy things to hide behind. Remind your children that the people with whom they are chatting and upon whom they are commenting are real people just like them. Just like words said in school, on the playground, or in the hallway can hurt, their online words can hurt too.

- **It is OK to disagree with someone's opinion. It is never appropriate to be rude, hateful, or mean because someone does not share your viewpoint.** We have told our children, "In life, you will never agree with someone all the time, not your parents, not a best friend, not your future spouse. It's how you treat them when you don't agree that defines your character."

"Kindness is the language which the deaf can hear and the blind can see." –Mark Twain.

- **Don't let negative comments on your pictures or posts, or even getting no likes at all, change how you feel about yourself.** This one is especially important to teach your girls. If you thought growing up pre-internet was tough with cliques (jocks, preppies, nerds), you wouldn't believe what your children endure with social media.

There has always been a silent code between mean girls and other "cliques" in school. Just because today's children spend most of the time online, that dynamic has not changed. It has only changed where and how the games are played. We have to remind children that who they are doesn't change because of how people see them online.

- **Don't get sucked into drama and refrain from starting any online.** Children today still have disagreements, except now they are displayed prominently online where everyone can see them. Teach your children to refrain from taking sides and posting. Encourage your children to come to you if they know something was posted that was not right. You can always pick up the phone and speak with the other parent offline. This could save your child and theirs some future digital grief.

- **Don't ever mention your location or where you go to school.** These days predators do not lure kids at the school bus nearly as much as they do online. Your children need to know what they should and should not be sharing. Please see the chapter on Predators for more information.

If there was one thing we wish parents truly grasped, it is that it does not matter if the information is inaccurate, it was just meant as a joke, or it was just a "kids being kids" prank. Once uploaded to social media, it is nearly impossible to erase or change and will have a lasting impact on your child's future, whether fair or not.

What You Can Do:

- Use monitoring programs. You will hear us repeat this throughout the book. You should not rely solely on parental controls. Parental controls are just one tool in your parenting toolbox. Take it from us. We know that most software can be circumvented by determined adversaries (your kids).

- While unpopular, hold off as long as you can with allowing children to get any social media accounts.

- Have ongoing discussions on appropriate social media behavior. You have to make time to talk with your children about social media. An easy way to do that is to be "online friends" with your children and talk about photos, comments, and other things that they post and that are posted by their friends. Ask questions such as:

  1. What did you think about what Susie posted?
  2. Would you have posted something different?
  3. Why did you like that? Why didn't you like it?
  4. How are your friends responding in real life to those pictures or that post?

What You Can Do:

- You want to engage your children and have conversations. You may not always like what they say or how they feel, but at least they are opening up and talking to you.

- Have rules and consequences. Make sure your children know what the appropriate behavior is and what the consequences are if/when they break the rules.

- Have social media "free" days. Play board games, watch a movie, walk around the mall and get pretzels or ice cream, or go to a sports game and talk. Read a book together out loud or build a LEGO set. Do things together with no posting, tweeting, snapping, or Insta-chatting. While you may not believe us, your kids will thank you later.

CHAPTER 9

Won't You Be My Friend?
Predators and Social Media

Melanie and her friends met at the mall every Thursday after school. They would grab a bite to eat at the food court, chat for a while, and then head off to their part-time jobs. Melanie, who was a "social" butterfly, would always snap a few photos and post them with the hashtags #everyThursday and #hangingB4work. Sounds like no big deal, right?

It was no big deal until the night that her brother didn't show up to get her after work and she was almost kidnapped.

One of her "friends" on social media was not really a friend. He was a 32-year-old registered sex offender who was stalking her and other girls her age in the area on social media.

Melanie was an easy target because she always posted where she was and what she was doing. All Tom, the predator, did was message Melanie's brother and tell him that he was going to bring Melanie home.

Melanie was lucky that night. She was smart enough to not get into the car with someone she had never met in real life. She was also fortunate that Tom did not turn into an aggressive maniac and grab her anyway.

You may think with kids spending more time online and less time outdoors that child kidnapping, exploitation, and other horrifying crimes against children would be rare. Unfortunately, that is not the case.

Personally, we are not fans of having children use social media. However, just because your child uses social media does not guarantee that your child will become a victim.

That is like saying riding a bicycle guarantees injury or death. While riding a bicycle can be dangerous, it matters where and how you are riding your bicycle. With social media, it matters how you are using it and what you are posting and sharing.

There are those who would suggest that parents who may be concerned with predators on social media are essentially uneducated and fearful because they do not understand this "new" world. One such example would be an article CNN ran entitled "Parents, Here's the Truth About Online Predators," by Christine Elgersma with Common Sense Media, in August of 2017.[36]

In this article, Ms. Elgersma goes on to tell parents that "While it's smart to be cautious, the facts show that it's actually fairly rare for kids to be contacted by adult strangers seeking sexual communication. Of course, it's natural to be concerned when your kid goes into an unknown world. But instead of acting out of fear, arm yourself with the facts so that you can help your kids be smart, cautious, and savvy."

While we agree with Ms. Elgersma saying that you should "arm yourself with facts so that you can help your kids be smart, cautious, and savvy," we disagree with her view that it is rare for kids to be contacted online by strangers.

One reason for our disagreement comes from the fact that she based her article on 2005 through 2010 data and statistics, during the early days of Facebook. Instagram began in October 2010 and Snapchat did not exist. Her assumption of "fairly rare" would be accurate for 2010, but not for today.

Here are the most recent statistics we could find:

- According to the Crimes Against Children Research Center, one in seven U.S. teenagers who regularly log on to the internet say they have received an unwanted sexual solicitation via the web.[37]

Solicitations were defined as requests to engage in sexual activities or sexual talk or to give out personal sexual information. (Only 25 percent of those teenagers told a parent.)

- Among children ages twelve through seventeen years old, 70 percent of girls and 30 percent of boys report being approached by a stranger while online.[38]

- In 2016 there were at least 53,552 child abuse/predator domains online; in 2017 there were at least 77,082—a 44 percent increase.[39]

(These sites are used to distribute pornography, sell kidnapped children, stalk children, share info, and trade tips and techniques on how to seduce and lure children into sexual encounters.)

- The Department of Homeland Security estimates that more than 500,000 sexual predators are online at any given moment.[40]

- According to the National Center for Missing and Exploited Children, CyberTipline reports of online enticement victims ranged in age from 1 to 17 years old.

In 2017 alone, the NCMEC received more than 10.2 million reports, a number that has been growing exponentially each year. The vast majority of reports (90%) involved offenders' direct communication with children, or an attempt to do so by either individual.

Children solicited directly by offenders were significantly older and less variable in age (Median = 15 years old; range = 6-17 years old) compared to children exploited as third-parties by/between offenders (Median = 11 years old; range = 1-17 years old).

Nearly all the children reported not knowing the extortioner except from online communications.[41]

The reality is that social media, chat rooms, and online gaming has made it easier for predators to pick targets.

From our research, there appear to be three main types of online predators. The first type would be what we call "The Pornographer." These individuals have no desire to meet children in real life. They only want to collect photos and/or videos of them and view them online.

Once they have a few photos of a child, they discontinue the relationship so that they are not caught. They will then either keep the photos private or they may post them to an online pornography site.

The second type we would call "The Sex Offenders." These individuals work to build trust and cultivate a relationship to the point that the child will meet face-to-face willingly, where they can have a physical interaction.

Individuals caught are normally charged with statutory rape for non-forcible sexual contact since most times the victims are by law too young to consent.

The U.S. Department of Justice National Sex Offender Public Website, Raising Awareness About Sexual Abuse, Facts and Statistics, states, "Of respondents to a survey of juvenile victims of Internet-initiated sex crimes, the majority met the predator willingly face-to-face, and 93 percent of those encounters had included sexual contact."[42]

The third type is a product of the new digital world (or social media world) that we live in today. We call them "Sextortioners." These individuals build trust and cultivate relationships and work to get children to give photos and/or videos that are sexual in nature. They then blackmail the child to continue sending photos and videos, which they in turn either sell or post on pornography sites.

Just so you are aware, there is a fourth type of online predator. There is no compiled data on them and they are supposedly in the minority. However, when they strike, it is tragic.

These are the predators that kidnap, rape, and then either sell a child as a sex slave (prostitute in the U.S. or overseas) or murder the child when they are done.

While the types of predators vary, they all share one common trait. They are master manipulators who can easily conceal themselves behind a keyboard and mouse. They pick up the subtle emotions in a child's post and then mirror those emotions, breaking down the wall of suspicion and building a camaraderie with the child.

A common example would be a child posting, "I really wanted those new Nike shoes. Can't believe Mom won't buy them!"

The online predator would post back, "I know, right?! Parents just don't get it. My mom wouldn't get me the new True Religion jeans…"

Most predators spend a lot of time working to break down the child's barriers. Once they believe the child is comfortable, they will test the waters by suggesting a sexual topic.

It could be a question as simple as, "Did you make out with John on your date?"

Remember, they have access to the child's social media account, so anything they have posted can assist with the "testing the water" questions. If they successfully make it past the first question, they just keep building the rapport until they either ask the child to send photos or videos or they take the relationship offline.

We believe the main reason that internet-initiated sex crimes against minors happen is that the relationship takes place in isolation and secrecy without societal norms. They are able to bond with the child because there is no oversight by family members, like meeting each other's parents or siblings or sitting down with the entire family for a meal. There is also no interaction with peers, such as going out to eat or to the movies with several groups of friends.

The absence of these societal norms at their young age builds an "it's me and you against the world" relationship/mentality, which usually leads to relationships that form more quickly, involve greater self-disclosure, and develop with greater intensity than traditional face-to-face relationships.

Most of the relationships that these predators build with young children have little to do with the child's lack of knowledge about sex and have more to do with finding their emotional insecurities, which they rarely discuss with their parents or adults in general.

One of the things you can do as a parent is try to maintain a solid bond with your child, even during the teenage years. Another thing you can do is keep in mind the doubts and insecurities that your child may be experiencing and work to find a way to offer guidance and talk about the issues.

Since most of us haven't been teenagers for a long time, here is a general list of what kids today voice as issues: being alone, rejected, not a part of the popular crew; having bad grades, not-good-enough-for-Mom-and-Dad grades, not-good-enough-for-college grades;

making mistakes, failing to achieve something, and therefore, disappointing one's friends, parents, teachers, or oneself; having the "wrong kind of" body, clothes, and hobbies.

How your child handles their own doubts and insecurities will affect how they interact with others, especially strangers online.

Online predators look for these three main types of social media behavior:

1. Posting personal information frequently. This would include using locations, Snap Map, and other information about where they are and what they are doing.

2. A large number of "friends" or "followers" on their social media accounts. This tells a predator that the child is open to people they do not know in real life.

3. Talking about sex or suggestive subjects online. This could be posting comments or suggestive images of themselves, as well as liking someone else's suggestive posts or images.

It is best to begin talking to your children about appropriate online behavior and the dangers of predators WAY BEFORE you give them devices and the ability to get online.

Back in the old days (pre-internet), this would be equivalent to teaching kids not to walk up to a car with a stranger in it who is asking for directions, or if they see a strange person following them, to run or go into a public building, such as a store or other place with a lot of people.

While predators still operate in the old-school manner, your children are far more likely to encounter a predator online. As a parent, it is up to you to make sure your children are prepared to protect themselves.

What You Can Do:

- Before your child starts with social media, set the ground rules. Discuss what is acceptable behavior and what the consequences will be if they choose not to follow the rules.

- Have a written social media contract with your child. Just like with their cell phone, a written agreement makes it very easy to say, "We agreed upon this, you broke the contract and so now you get to live with the consequences."

- Use social media monitoring software. This will alert you to inappropriate comments or content that your child may post.

- Be clear on what information they should never post, such as sexual comments, where they live, where they work, etc.

- Let them know that if a "friend" or "follower" that they haven't met in real life or with whom they don't go to school starts asking personal questions or questions that are sexual in nature, they should come talk to you or another adult in their lives. Remind them that you won't be angry with them, you love them, and want to make sure that they are safe.

- Monitor your child's online activity. Don't rely solely on monitoring tools if you are using them. Not only should you

What You Can Do:

have every password to every social media site, they should know that you will be checking in on them. Predators find children primarily through social media. This can start with a friend request, a dialogue on a chat or game forum, or using a video platform like Omegle.

• There is software available that will not allow the use of social media without parental permission, as well as block access to adult content. If you do not want your child using social media, by all means, this is the way to go.

However, that does not exempt the need to have open conversations with your children about digital safety. *Kids can buy pay-as-you-go phones and surf free public Wi-Fi available just about everywhere these days, going wherever they want online **without** their parents' knowledge.*

• Have ongoing open conversations about online safety. Today's kids are much smarter than you when it comes to technology (unless you are an IT professional/hacker). If they really wanted to, most kids could find a way around the monitoring apps you put in place.

What You Can Do:

- Review your kids "friends" with your child at least every other month. Remove all the friends of friends that they don't know and have never met in real life. If every other month is too often for you, a review every six months should be a minimum.

- Sit with your children while they play their games. Parents are shocked to know that even simple games like Minecraft have online predators, and not just on social media.

  Most children think that all players are OK to talk to, and they converse innocently without knowing that they are already giving away their personal information to potential cyber stalkers. You may also be shocked at some of the dialogue you see in some of these games.

CHAPTER 10

The Dark Side of Gaming: Addiction, Porn, and Bullying

Remember when games were played outside and Pac-Man was considered high-tech? Remember when you had to go to the arcade to play the latest video games? Kids today carry the arcade around with them in their pockets, and today's video game visuals mimic real life.

Children today play video games with friends around the block and strangers around the world, thanks to the internet. Many adults also participate in this new online gaming world. Anyone with a game console, computer, and internet can put on a headset, turn on a webcam, and talk to and play with any of the millions of gamers around the world.

The U.S. video game industry generated more than $30

billion in revenue in 2016, according to the Entertainment Software Association and the NPD Group.[43] The entire video gaming industry generated $108.4 billion in revenue in 2017.[44]

In a *Los Angeles Times* article by David Lazarus[45] entitled, "Are video games bad for your kids? Not so much, experts now believe," he stated:

"At a recent seminar on video games at UC Irvine, Constance Steinkuehler, a professor of informatics at the school and president of the Higher Education Video Game Alliance, emphasized that most researchers embrace the idea that 'play is good.' She also acknowledged that video games, like smartphones, social media, and other modern technologies, can have addictive properties.

I spoke with Steinkuehler this week and she said, 'There's a lot of confusion and a lot of fear' among parents as to how they should respond to an interest that's consuming much of their kids' lives. Many kids are spending more time on average playing games than they are on homework.'

Yes, games can be addictive in some cases, she said. But, no, there isn't any meaningful evidence that video games lead to abhorrent or violent behavior."

There are two interesting things that parents should know here before we jump into the technology dangers of gaming. One, online video gaming, including the latest VR (virtual reality) glasses, is a huge **BILLION**-dollar industry. As with any industry of this size, they "fund" colleges, departments, and educators' programs and studies. Most people would be hard-pressed to intentionally bite the hand that feeds them.

The second interesting note for parents in the area of gaming is that The National Center for Biotechnology Information has been publishing medical studies on the effects of internet gaming on the brain since 2012. *A lot of them.*

As of the writing of this book, there are more than 3,030 medical studies on the effects of gaming, social media, and internet use and what it does to a child's brain. In 2018 alone, the number of *published* medical studies is at 527! I will not even tell you the hours I have spent reading medical "research" papers—it is really a good thing that I enjoy reading!

The basic consensus of all the brain imaging studies and research to date is: prolonged gaming, social media, and internet use has the same effect on the brain as prolonged substance (drug/alcohol) use.

In layman's terms, the result is that children can become addicted to the games and yet believe that they don't have a gaming problem. If you would like to review these studies, some of the reference links are included in the end of the book—happy reading![46]

We want to be honest and say that we are not completely anti-games. Our four children have a great time battling with the Just Dance and Karaoke games. We watch them play and all laugh hysterically. It is great fun. Our kids also have a PS4 (PlayStation) on which they play the Star Wars BattleFront games, but it lives in the living room, they play about twice a month, and there are no chat functions.

We know there is a darker side and real dangers like cyberbullying, pornography, and online predators. There is also the teaching of wasteful spending on in-game purchases (weapons, provisions, and "skins").

There are a multitude of items about which to be concerned if your children are gaming. We are going to cover what we consider the top three dangers.

1. Cyber bullying. Games allow kids to escape from real life and into a world where they can be anything (monster, zombie, alien) or anyone (superhero, gangster, tycoon). It is a place where no one knows what they look like or who they are in real life. Some players take advantage of this anonymous identity. They do things to other players that intentionally make the game less enjoyable and normally turns into bullying.

In gaming, instead of "bullies" they are called "griefers." It is even in the dictionary!

The Urban Dictionary actually has the following examples[47]:

- Player versus player abuse: Singling out the same person and killing them over and over when they are defenseless until they log off.

- Kill stealing: Repeatedly trying to steal another person's kills so that their time is wasted.

- Verbal abuse: Spamming a person with vulgar, hateful, or offensive messages.

- Blocking: Getting in another's way so they cannot move or get out of a particular area.

- Training: Triggering many monsters, almost always impossible to fight and survive, with the intention to either run someone out of an area or kill them indirectly if the server is not "player versus player" enabled.

2. Pornography. Pornography can be accessed from any device with a web browser and an internet connection. It is just as easy to access porn on your Smart TV and your gaming consoles (Nintendo, Xbox, and the Virtual Reality products such as the Oculus Rift owned by Facebook) as it is with your laptop, tablet, and smartphone.

In 2018, the traffic going to Pornhub (the largest pornography site on the internet) from gaming consoles was as follows: 62 percent from PlayStation devices and 33 percent from Xbox devices.[48]

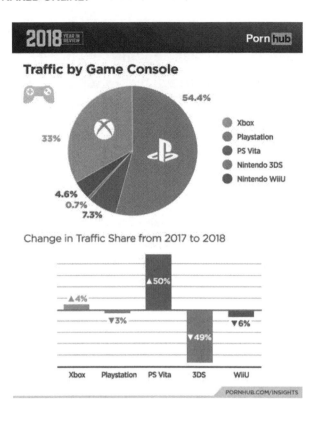

More and more games have pornography embedded in them, from the way the characters look to scenes in the games. What most of your kids know, that you most likely do not, is that there is also pornography based on their favorite games, and believe me, the stats say they are looking.

Fortnite tops the list for game pornography searches. If you don't know much about Fortnite, you may want to read the article "How Fortnite Captured Teens' Hearts and Minds," by Nick Paumgarten. It was in the May 21, 2018, issue of *The New Yorker*.

This article goes on to describe how addictive the game is,

and gives the comparison to the Beatlemania craze of the 1960's, the opioid crisis, and eating Tide Pods. You can also find this article online—it is a very interesting read for parents.[49]

MindGeek, which also owns Pornhub, YouPorn, and adult film studios and serves as the online operating partner for *Playboy*, has taken a cue from the standard gaming industry and started a free-to-play game platform that is designed to attract younger adults and kids.

Prior to 2017, all the online adult games required a credit card for an initial purchase as well as the ongoing monthly subscription fee, also known as a "paywall". The defenders of online porn games stated that "paywalls and monthly subscriptions" prevented access by children.

MindGeek launching **free-to-play** porn games online, saying children will not be able to access the games, is a joke and an insult on any intelligent parent. Just the words "free-to-play" say it all.

Then there is the "adult" virtual reality market that uses headsets, such as the Oculus Rift, where in just a few clicks, your tech-savvy child can have apps downloaded. However, with the Oculus Rift, many of the "adult" games are streaming only.

All your kid needs is an internet connection and they can delete the icon after playing so there is no trace of where they were or what they were doing.

Gone are the days of only worrying about magazines hidden under beds and stuffed in dresser drawers.

We recommend that you set up parental controls on gaming consoles and review any game prior to your children getting full access. If you want to seriously protect your children, you need professional equipment that your smart kids cannot go around.

3. Personal information left on game consoles and computers. When they have outlived their usefulness, or the newest greatest edition arrives at Christmas, many families donate these devices to their local Goodwill, take them to a consignment store, or sell them on swap sites. Parents and older children often forget to delete their files and personal information, in turn putting their financial and private lives at risk.

You should find a professional to help you remove all data from these devices before you donate or recycle them. Some devices require special tools or procedures to ensure that all the data is removed and cannot be retrieved.

Before we close this chapter, we would like to give you one last tip. This one is specifically for you, the parent. This has to do with the "free-to-play" games.

Be aware that many of these games will use the credit card

you have on file for your iTunes or Google Play account. If your child clicks on any of the optional in-app purchases or upgrades, your credit card is automatically charged.

You should disable in-app purchases to prevent your children from racking up huge credit card bills for games without even realizing it. This recently happened to someone we know. Their son racked up over $10,000 on "in-app" purchases in two months of playing just a single game.

We strongly believe that by limiting a child's access to gaming, they are more likely to find joy in real-world activities, such as spending time with family, reading, creative endeavors, and school. This also helps children learn that technology is best used as a tool, not a toy.

Warning: the following is a strong personal opinion about games. If you are easily offended, please skip this and head straight to the "What You Can Do" section. Don't say we didn't warn you.

Those in the gaming industry sound a lot like the tobacco companies of yester-year. "Smoking is good for you!" they proclaimed in the 1950s and 1960s.

Then when the reality started to show that smoking was not so healthy, the tobacco companies were forced to label their products with "Smoking may be hazardous to your health."

Now that there is concrete evidence that smoking causes cancer, shortens your lifespan, and results in a whole host of other really bad things, the tobacco companies have warning labels like: "Smoking causes cancer and lung disease" and "Don't smoke if you are pregnant..."

The tobacco industry and the gaming industry both make *a lot* of money. They also operate under the same guiding principles.

Their job is not to protect their users. Their job is to get their users hooked, for life, so that they can bring in profit, stay in business, and collect a paycheck or payout hefty dividends.

We believe that eventually what we saw with the tobacco companies and their warnings is what we will see with the gaming industry.

We are just now at the phase where the experts in the industry are quietly admitting: "Gaming may be hazardous (addictive) to your child's health and causes brain damage."

What You Can Do:

- Check your child's game console settings. Most game consoles have parental control options, make sure you take advantage of them.

- Check to see if your child's games allow players to "block" chat and messages from other users. If so, consider turning that feature on. They can still play the game; they just will not see the dialogue.

- Teach your children to never give away any kind of personal information in their gaming worlds.

- Have different user names and passwords for your child across different games and gaming sites. This keeps hackers and predators from being able to connect the social dots of who they are and where they live.

- Talk with your child about the games they are playing. We encourage you to sit and play the game or sit and watch your child play the game.

In many cases, predators seek to turn kids against their parents by taking up the mantle of they are the "only person who really

What You Can Do:

understands them." If you are actively involved with your child's game time, an online predator will not stand a chance with them.

- Don't just throw out, donate, or sell your used game console, tablet, phone, or computer. You should wipe all personal data and then perform a factory reset.

  The specific tools or procedures needed vary depending on the age and type of device, so it is important to have a professional take care of this for you. *This is one time that doing it yourself is not worth the risk.*

- Use a low-limit credit card or get a reloadable gift Visa card for games. The last thing you want to see is a $10,000 credit card bill because your children wanted to get to level 21 on their favorite "free" game.

- Even if your child is playing more traditional subscription-based games, it is a good idea to regularly check your credit card bills to make sure you are not being charged for purchases you did not agree to make.

What You Can Do:

- Get professional-grade network equipment in your home. Your tech-savvy kids or their friends can go around pretty much anything you purchase at Best Buy, Amazon, or any local store.

  It's a small price to pay to protect your children from pornography, predators, and other places they shouldn't be online. It's also really not that expensive if done right.

- Keep all gaming consoles in the family room, den or other room where everyone lives. Kids who keep their gaming systems in their bedroom are more likely to stay up late, venture into dangerous conversations and surf pornography websites.

CHAPTER 11

Who's Afraid of the Big Bad Cyber Bully?

Joe, a high school football player, just asked Stephanie, a pretty brunette who is a science geek, out on a date. While Stephanie liked Joe as a person, she was not interested in him romantically, so she said, "No thanks."

Upset by Stephanie's rejection, on Thursday evening Joe and a few of his buddies pulled two pornographic photos off the internet, wrote Stephanie's name on them, and sent the images to the football team's Snapchat group.

By Friday afternoon, the post had more than three hundred comments and had been shared more than five hundred times. It had also found its way onto Instagram and Facebook.

Stephanie was now the subject of crude comments and death threats—over photos that were not even of her.

Joe and his gang of accomplices admitted to school officials and the police that the images are not Stephanie's and that they found them randomly online. However, for Stephanie, the damage is done. The rumors persist, even though she has shut off all her social media accounts. There are constant whispers behind her back, in the bathroom, in the hallways, even at the mall and restaurants outside of school.

These pictures are never going away. The thought that a potential employer in five years might be able to find these images is devastating and starts Stephanie down the path of self-harming, depression, and several attempts to end her life.

Little did Stephanie know that by just saying "no" to that date, her life would change forever.

Joe and his friends were removed from the football team and each given a one-week suspension, which in comparison to their crime, seems like a wink and a small slap on the wrist.

This same story plays out in various forms and degrees every day across America, with most parents in the dark and most schools at a loss for how to handle it or discipline for it.

All fifty states have zero-tolerance policies to prevent bullying in schools, but for most cases, school officials give little more than lip service to them.

How are they supposed to keep up with everything that every child in every grade is saying online? Really, it is an impossible task.

If your child is being bullied, you should go to the school immediately with all the proof, including text messages, screen shots, and anything else.

If your school officials ignore or brush off the incident, please go to the police. Do not wait; your child's life might depend on it.

In the pre-internet days, bullying usually consisted of spreading rumors about people, keeping certain people out of a "group," teasing people in a mean way, and getting certain people to "gang up" on others. Sometimes there was physical bullying, but it was rare.

Today's children face a new frontier in bullying—cyber bullying. Unlike the bullying of the past, cyber bullying (also called digital bullying) never goes away. It lives forever online for everyone to see.

Suicide is now the second leading cause of death in children ages ten to twenty-four.[50] It seems very coincidental that the statistics coincide with the increased use of social media. The constant pressure to be the best online and show how "fabulous" your life is has created jealousy, which fuels cyber bullying.

According to StopBullying.gov, more than 70 percent of young people say they have seen bullying in their schools, and almost 30 percent of U.S. students in grades 6 through 12 have experienced cyber bullying.[51]

For those of you who may not be familiar with cyber bullying, it generally consists of sending mean texts, e-mails, or instant messages; posting nasty pictures or messages about others online (blogs, forums, social media sites); using someone else's username or "catfishing" (creating fake accounts) to spread rumors or lies about someone.

It is important that you and your children know that cyber bullying is serious. The school could expel your child and they could be charged with manslaughter if another student commits suicide because of their bullying.

There are numerous lawsuits where a family is suing the school along with the student or students (if it was a group effort) who bullied a child that committed suicide. There are already cases where children have been convicted of involuntary manslaughter, setting the precedent for children to be held accountable for their digital words.

The base sentence for involuntary manslaughter under federal sentencing guidelines is a ten- to sixteen-month prison sentence, which increases if the crime was committed through an act of reckless conduct.

While the criminal charges are life altering, the mental damage of living the rest of their life knowing that the words they said caused someone to end their life is much worse. There is no punishment that will erase that knowledge.

Today's children spend most of their time on Snapchat and Instagram. Both of these social media platforms make it easy for tech-savvy kids to set up new anonymous or fake profiles that their parents do not know about.

According to a 2017 survey conducted by Ditch the Label, a nonprofit anti-bullying group, more than one in five kids ages twelve to twenty years old experience bullying, specifically on Instagram.[52]

As we mentioned before, the majority of bullying stems from jealousy, and Instagram is the ultimate jealousy platform. Many kids are constantly posting pictures of their cars, their new clothes, and their bodies, trying to one-up their peers and compete with the Kardashians.

Instagram, just like Facebook, will remove posts that they deem are in violation of their policies. Any blatant bullying will get

ARE YOUR KIDS NAKED ONLINE?

your Instagram account deleted.

Kids today are smart, and they know how to game the system. Therefore, you will not find much bullying on the main Instagram feed. Most bullying takes place over direct message, Instagram Stories, or in the comments section of friends' photos.

In an effort to reduce cyber bullying, some schools have instituted a device-free policy. Phones are prohibited while on campus. Students must check in their device when they get to school and they can pick up their device when the school day is complete. If a parent really needs to get in touch with a student, they can call the school directly.

While we applaud these schools for taking action, unfortunately the rules do not curb bullying. The kids just launch their attacks after school.

Social networking sites like Facebook, Instagram, Twitter, and Snapchat are actually weapons, and as a parent, you should think of them as such.

They can be used for good and for evil. Whether we like it or not, they give individuals a special "power" that allows them to say what they want, to whomever they want, whenever they want, and they are able to hide behind a cloak of anonymity and destroy others' futures and sometimes take their lives.

What You Can Do:

- Start early! If you have four- to five-year-olds, you should be teaching them about bullying and how to treat others with our words and actions.

- Talk to your children about the ramifications of being a cyber bully. Discuss the schools' rules and consequences, as well as how it could impact their future, including their college and career decisions. Depending on the age of your child, you may want to share specific examples of what can happen.

- Encourage your children not to boast on social media, by posts or photos.

- Review your school's policies as well as your state's laws on bullying. You want to know what the consequences are for being a bully and what the rights are if your child is the one being bullied.

- Let your children know there is no shame in being the target of a cyber bully. Encourage them to talk to you. The worst thing you can do as a parent is fly off the handle on this topic or underestimate how the words are affecting your child.

What You Can Do:

- Teach your children as soon as you can that they should not share anything about themselves that they would not want posted on the biggest billboard in town with their picture on it.

- Remind your teenagers that they should not say anything that they do not want their grandparents (or favorite relative who they admire) to see. Again, think of the billboard analogy.

- If your child has been bullied, you may want to seek professional help from someone they can talk to that is not a family member or in their school.

  As parents, we understand the thought that our children should just talk to us; however, our children do not always feel the same way. If your child does not want to talk to you, please, try to find someone with whom they will be comfortable talking that can help them.

- As we have mentioned in prior chapters, you should have the passwords for your children's social media accounts, and you should be a friend and follower of all their social media accounts.

What You Can Do:

- Use a monitoring program. The reality is that kids should have no expectation of privacy. They are KIDS. You are not spying, you are parenting. This one thing could help prevent a tragedy, either in your family or someone else's.

CHAPTER 12

The Dark Web: What It Is, What It's Not

Ryan looks like any other fourteen-year-old in his school. He is athletic, funny, and gets along with everyone. He also has a side business. He buys drugs on the dark web for himself and his classmates.

His parents only learned about his business because they opened a package that should have been books from Amazon. Instead of books, they found a sealed bag of cannabis (marijuana) and several bags of pills.

According to Ryan, they were "Molly" (aka Ecstasy/MDMA), a popular drug with kids today, especially in the electronic dance music scene.

Ryan explained, "It was easy to purchase, easier to sell, and

I could earn money without working at a 'real' job after school. I downloaded Tor on to my computer, Googled 'drugs' and bingo—there were hundreds of sites. I already have $13,500 in the bank!"

The dark web largely was the brainchild of Paul Syverson, David Goldschlag, and Michael Reed, three mathematicians at the Naval Research Laboratory, as a means of encrypting messages exchanged by the intelligence community. They dubbed their project "Tor," for "The Onion Router," as the system consists of layer after layer of random relays, permitting anonymity on the Internet with little risk of tracking or surveillance. It was actually created with good intentions, and as with many good things, can and is being used for illegal activity and evil.

The easiest analogy to keep it simple is to look at the internet like an iceberg. You can see so much on top of the water and you can also see that it extends below the water, but unless you venture into the water you have no way of knowing how deep the iceberg goes, but you know it does go deep.

In the case of the internet, it has three main parts and works like this:
1. The surface web. This is the public internet we use every day and access through standard browsers like Chrome, Internet Explorer, Safari, etc.

2. The deep web. This is not accessible via your public browser.

The majority of the deep web is neither dark nor dangerous. It primarily consists of government archives, medical records, or an organization's internal communications system (knowledge bases or wikis).

3. The dark web. This is very dangerous, especially for children. It can only be accessed through a secret system of servers that exists separately from the public internet, and only special browsers can let you in. This part of the internet is a portal into a world in which identity ceases to exist.

Note: You will hear and read that the surface web is 4 percent, the deep web is 90 percent, and the dark web is 6 percent, or some numbers close to those. We have intentionally left those numbers out due to no one really knowing the extent of the deep or dark web.

The dark web can invade any home at any time, and it entices teens into a world of porn, drugs, and other illegal and hidden dangers.

Parents often ask, "How do kids get to the dark web?"

The surface web is loaded with information on how to access the dark web. There are even forums that provide tips on which program is best and how to navigate through the dark web.

With just a few clicks, kids can venture into a dangerous abyss giving them access to sites such as Hidden Wiki, the Uncensored Hidden Wiki, the deep web Links, and many others. On these sites, kids will find child pornography, weapons, fake documents, drugs, and even recruitment by terrorists.

Something to keep in mind: when your kids are surfing the dark web, it resembles the surface web's shopping sites, with product descriptions, photos, and buyer and seller feedback. There are no skulls, crossbones, and other images that come to your mind when you think of the "scary dark web." Well, there are those sites, but they do not make up the majority of dark web sites.

The dark web not only connects kids with suppliers, but it also allows them to pay for the drugs and products using payment networks like Bitcoin.

If you have not heard of Bitcoin, it is an open peer-to-peer financial network that uses untraceable digital currency and is the payment of choice for dark web merchandise and services.

Once a transaction has been processed, dark-world merchants cleverly conceal, package, and ship the product out using everyday shipping services like the U.S. Postal Service, UPS, or FedEx.

There is one other area of the dark web we would like you as a parent to know about if you don't already. It's a website that is called Sanctioned Suicide, and its professed mission and reason for "being" is to give anyone a safe and completely anonymous haven to talk about their darkest thoughts. There are also people on the forum who freely give advice on how to find a suitable way of choosing to end their own lives, if that is their desire.

Our kids deal with an enormous amount of stress, between their grades, getting into the right college, dating the right person, and having the right clothes, and compounded by the nonstop online social façade they must keep up, it is reasonable to assume that they may experience bad days and sometimes bad thoughts and perhaps need someone to talk to.

While I'm sure you're saying, "They can come talk to me," most kids are not likely to do that. So they turn to the dark web where they can be anonymous and chat without judgment, and this site preys on their vulnerability.

One of the first publicized suicides attributed to the Sanctioned Suicide forum is that of Leilani Clarke, a sixteen-year-old student in the U.K. whose disappointing mock exam results sent her to the suicide chatroom on the dark web.[53] The next morning, her mother found her dead.

There is more to the dark web than just purchasing illegal drugs.

Here are just a few other things your kids can do on the dark web:

- Purchase a fake ID (used to get into dance clubs or buy alcohol for parties)

- Obtain illegal weapons at any age

- Hire a hitman for you,[54] any other adults, or their enemies at school

- Hire a hacker hitman[55] to ruin an adult or their enemies at school

- Book a child sex holiday or sign up to participate in one

- Attempt to have an enemy kidnapped and sold into a sex ring

While the dark web is still used for some good, for kids there is nothing but evil to be found.

What You Can Do:

- Let your middle and high school children know that a drug charge can disqualify them from college grants and loans, keep them from serving in the military, and impede their search for employment, as well as prevent them from working in some industries (finance/medical/legal just to name a few), or prohibit them from obtaining a professional license. For some children, just knowing this might give them a moment's pause.

- Talk with your kids about the issues that they are facing. Please do not tell your child, "I went through it too; everybody goes through it, and you'll come out of it OK." Keep in mind, while you (we) all had peer pressure, we were not living in a "24/7/365 everything is posted online about us" social world.

- If you think your child is upset or depressed, offer to help them find someone to talk to if they do not want to talk with you. Let them know that you understand they don't want to talk with you (even if you really don't understand) and reach out to someone who can help them: a trusted counselor, a church member, or a local support group in your area that is reputable. This is not the time to be prideful about your child not wanting to talk to you.

What You Can Do:

- Have open conversations with your kids about what the dark web is and how it is used. Start as EARLY as you can, say between seven and eight years old. One Google search on "kids on the dark web" will give you plenty of examples of kids who have gone to jail, ruined their lives, been kidnapped, sold into sex rings, or killed themselves all after visiting the dark web. You can share these and use them as lessons with your kids.

- Check your child's phones and devices periodically for unusual web browsers. Some of the normal browsers are Safari, Chrome, Internet Explorer, and Firefox. If you think your child has something out of the ordinary, you may want to contact an IT professional to help you remove it.

- Use monitoring software that will alert you if any of these browsers or virtual private networks (VPNs) have been installed.

- Have a business grade firewall at home that can filter and block specific internet traffic, certain websites and certain web browsers.

CHAPTER 13

Tech Giants: Do as I Say, Not as I Do

It is no secret that Bill Gates and Steve Jobs, two of the world's most iconic tech leaders, restricted and banned their children from using the same technology that they created and were pushing on the rest of the world.

Now you may be thinking, "Well, those guys are old, what about the younger group of tech leaders? Like Google, Facebook, Instagram, and others?" Interesting thought, glad you asked.

There is a school in Silicon Valley that has a total of nine classrooms and there is not an iPad, smartphone, or screen of any type in sight. This school is where the chief technology officer of eBay sends his children, as well as employees of Google, Apple, Yahoo, and Hewlett-Packard. Not only are there no "devices" in the school, this school actually frowns on the children using them at home!

What school in America today would have such restrictions? The Waldorf Schools. Particularly, The Waldorf School of the Peninsula, where most of the tech world sends its children.

So if all this technology is so great, why would the people who created it want to keep their own children from it? Why would most people in the technology industry, us included, keep our children from it until they are much older?

While none of the Silicon Valley tech leaders have come out and written an in-depth article on their decisions, especially since they have shareholders and profits to consider, here are the top three reasons that we have pieced together from the information we have read, comments they have said openly, and information that we personally know.

1. It is designed to be addictive—intentionally. Have you ever started playing a game only to look up and realize you have just spent thirty minutes or an hour playing that game? (For Lisa and several of our children, real books have that same effect.)

It is intentional. Games and social media challenge you, some tell you a story, and others let you tell a story (Facebook and Instagram), some put you in control of whole worlds and, like a good book or TV series, they all present compelling reasons for you to stay engaged.

Many of the companies that design technology and games have psychologists on staff that specialize in the fields of persuasive design and how to influence behavior through media.

Did you know that Stanford University has a course called "Computer Systems: How to Design Addictive Games"? And the rest of the colleges that offer "gaming" degrees have similar courses.

There has not been a recent true comprehensive study on how much time kids spend online. The last study I could find is the Common Sense Media Study from 2015, which stated, "Teenagers (ages 13-18) use an average of nine hours of entertainment media per day and tweens (ages 8-12) use an average of six hours a day, not including time spent using media for school or homework."[56]

From what we can tell, the reason there hasn't been a more recent study of how much time kids are spending in their electronic media is because many of the companies providing the survey results are funded by many of the major tech companies. So what company is going to publish data that would portray their largest investors in a negative light and thereby bite the hand that feeds them?

While I am sure someone has the real data, I do not believe that most parents are ready for that truth. Besides, the social media companies only want to provide your data to people who will pay them money. You don't really think Facebook, Instagram, and Snapchat are free, do you?

Their main concern is not to protect or make your children's lives better. Their main goal is to get your kids hooked and loyal to their platform/brand/app as soon as possible.

This is our personal opinion with what we see around us through family and friends; we would estimate that most children spend five to six hours a day online, not counting school and homework. When we say "online," we mean, texting, playing games, and on social media platforms. Our estimate is most likely conservative.

Ask yourself, what are your children missing, or what could they be doing if they were not spending five to six hours a day of their free time playing games or on social media?

These are some of the things that fill the "online" void at our house: LEGOs, spending time with their eighty-seven-year-old great granny, reading the classics (*Livy's History of Rome* or *Plutarch's Lives*), reading current books of all kinds, fishing, learning how to write marketing copy (thank you, Dan Kennedy), designing beautiful gift bags and selling them, trying out new recipes in the kitchen, writing original stories, as well as learning how to grocery shop and create a budget. You get the idea.

Here are some excerpts taken from the October 26, 2018, *The*

New York Times online article: "A Dark Consensus About Screens and Kids Begins to Emerge in Silicon Valley," by Nellie Bowles[57]:

For longtime tech leaders, watching how the tools they built affect their children has felt like a reckoning on their life and work.

Among those is Chris Anderson, the former editor of Wired and now the chief executive of a robotics and drone company. He is also the founder of GeekDad.com. "On the scale between candy and crack cocaine, it's closer to crack cocaine," Mr. Anderson said of screens.

Technologists building these products and writers observing the tech revolution were naïve, he said. "We thought we could control it," Mr. Anderson said. "And this is beyond our power to control. This is going straight to the pleasure centers of the developing brain. This is beyond our capacity as regular parents to understand."

Those who have exposed their children to screens try to talk them out of addiction by explaining how the tech works. John Lilly, a Silicon Valley-based venture capitalist with Greylock Partners and the former C.E.O. of Mozilla, said he tries to help his 13-year-old son understand that he is being manipulated by those who built the technology. "I try to tell him somebody wrote code to make you feel this way—I'm trying to help him understand how things are made, the values that are going into things and what people are doing to create that feeling," Mr. Lilly said. "And he's like, 'I just

157

want to spend my 20 bucks to get my Fortnite skins.'"

What social media and gaming are doing is having children give up their childhood. They are taking time that should be filled with laughter, fun, stretching and trying new things, falling down and failing, and learning about real life, and replacing it with Fortnite, Minecraft, Instagram, and YouTube.

When something is addictive, you do not consider its negative effects; you just want more of it.

2. The Loss of Communication Skills. We are the first to admit that technology has given us the ability to connect with more people in ways that would not be possible without it.

I have a weekly Zoom meeting with colleagues who live in Virginia, Boston, Atlanta, California, New York, and London. It is wonderful to see their faces and not just hear their voices over the telephone or read their words in a letter.

However, one of the downsides of technology, especially for children today, is that it impairs their ability to detect the emotions of other people. Kids that spend the majority of their time with screens and devices have a difficult time reading people's nonverbal cues, which in real life with real people are essential.

They use emojis to express their feelings, and they prefer to communicate via abbreviated text messages through the phone or social media, even if they are in the same room with the other person.

The other down side is their inability to hold a conversation or pay attention—in real life with real people.

Does it bother you when you are talking to another person and they pull out their phone and start checking their email or texting?

Really, what is your first thought? My first thought is, "I must be so boring or I'm not important enough for this person to give me their full attention." Unfortunately, most children, as well as millennials who grew up on technology, are guilty of this behavior. We also know quite a few baby boomers who are guilty of this behavior!

Here is an example that happened to Lisa. I was at a speaking conference in New York when the individual from the company who put on the conference engaged me in conversation and asked me a question.

As I started to answer his question, he pulled out his phone and began checking email or some other task. He did not even realize that I stopped talking to him mid-sentence, and then he walked away, oblivious to the fact that I stopped talking to him and never answered his question! I was actually dumbfounded and shocked.

My first thought was, "If he wasn't interested in being present while we talked, WHY did he bother to come over and ask me the question?"

And my second thought was, "Well, I guess to him I'm not that important to talk to."

While this may sound like no big deal, this conference was designed to get interested individuals to sign up for a new program, and they lost me from that moment on.

3. Bad Behavior, Delusion, and Narcissism. We call bad behavior, delusion, and narcissism the trifecta of technology games and social media.

We will start with bad behavior. Have you ever been in a restaurant where a parent took a device away from a child? I am sure that some of you are laughing now because you know exactly what I am talking about.

Depending on their age, you will either witness a screaming opera show, a murder by facial expressions, arms crossed and the "I hate you and wish you were dead" look, or a combination of the two.

We wish we could say that is the only place bad behavior happens, but it is not. In homes all across the world, doors are slammed, items are picked up and thrown, and children yell and scream, "I hate you, I want to play my game!" or "I can't wait until

I'm old enough to leave, then I can do whatever I want online!" as they stomp to their room.

There is also bad behavior toward others online. Bullying those they don't like.

Next up is delusion and narcissism. These two go together like the wicked stepsisters from *Cinderella*. You may see them exhibited by a child with online gaming, but they really rear their heads once a child is actively engaged in social media. It's sad to say, but adults too are not immune from this behavior.

Some of you may be thinking, "My child is on social media and we don't have that problem."

To which I say, "We realize that there are exceptions to this; however, this is more the norm than the exception." We would also advise you to reevaluate what you think you see.

Kids today are digitally self-obsessed. When they aren't watching and reading posts by celebrities, friends, and frenemies, they are spending their time crafting the perfectly angled photos and writing snappy captions.

Lying in the real world can get them into trouble. However, lying or exaggerating on social media gets them likes, comments, followers, and a sense of fame.

They know that their "candid" photos were expertly staged, took eight attempts, that they Facetuned their teeth to be whiter, their waist and thighs to be thinner, and their hair to be lighter.

These children start to believe their own illusions. They are self-made celebrities where they are actors in their own fictionalized stories. They will turn on anyone who dares to contradict this illusion—from blocking people, unfollowing, and bullying, to spreading nasty rumors to quench their jealousy.

They are creating a fake sense of self that sets them up for depression. If you do not believe me, ask a teenager how they feel about a photo they posted that had hundreds of "likes." Then ask the same teenager how they feel about a photo they posted that got zero likes or no attention at all.

All social media platforms are comprised of individuals and now companies, competing against each other for followers, likes, retweets, favorites, and whatever other "terms" of approval exist out there in social media land.

We recommend that all parents read these two *New York Times* articles written by Nellie Bowles: "The Digital Gap Between Rich and Poor Kids Is Not What We Expected" and "A Dark Consensus About Screens and Kids Begins to Emerge in Silicon Valley."

These articles touch on the elephant in the room that no one wants to discuss in depth. Why are the people who invent all this "great" technology sending their kids to schools where there is NO technology and then restricting or banning it in their homes?

Some may call the articles extreme or alarmist, but as technology professionals and parents ourselves, we found them informative and reinforced a great deal of what we have personally thought for years, with a few caveats.

Ms. Bowles' articles are written from a class warfare perspective, which we do not agree with. The reality is, employees at *all levels* of these tech companies are sending their kids to device-free schools or are homeschooling.

This issue is about the appropriateness of children using technology and how it changes their brain development. It affects their creativity, ability to think logically, and their ability to interact with other humans. That is the real issue and the driving reason behind why tech giants and others in the industry have opted their young children out.

There is a time for children to learn technology; they just do not believe it is from kindergarten to eighth grade. From ninth grade to twelfth grade, it's used when necessary as a tool.

Whatever your political persuasion, or feelings about children and technology, the fifteen minutes it would take you to read these two articles is well worth the time spent. Also ask yourself, if you took away all your child's devices for a full forty-eight hours (Saturday and Sunday), what kind of rebellion would you have on your hands?

What's a parent to do? We get it: not everyone can send their children to a private school, nor does everyone want to homeschool their children. We also realize that the world is never going back to the way it was before smartphones, online games, and social media existed.

As parents, we have to ask ourselves these questions:

1. When should our children be given technology and what is the purpose of giving it?

2. What type of technology do they really need?

3. How do we teach them to use this technology in a healthy way and not let it rule their lives?

4. Am I using technology in a way that models the behavior I want my children to model? Remember, more is caught than taught. You can't get by with "Do as I say, not as I do."

The "What You Can Do" section of this chapter includes suggestions and possible products that you may want to implement at home to balance out your child's technology use, especially if they are using devices every day in school. Even implementing a few of these suggestions will benefit your child and help them in the future.

164

"I think also, that general virtue is more probably to be expected and obtained from the education of youth, than from the exhortation of adult persons; bad habits and vices of the mind, being, like diseases of the body, more easily prevented than cured." - Benjamin Franklin, August 23, 1750, from The Papers of Benjamin Franklin, Vol. 4

What You Can Do:

- Institute a book-of-the-month reading plan. Even if your child already reads, we suggest adding a book of the month that is a biography. Have them mix up the types of biographies they read; don't let them just read biographies of celebrities or individuals they identify with. While we do not recommend this, we have a friend who gives "extra" game time for every book their child reads and writes a report on. She says, "Sometimes the dangling carrot is necessary."

- If your child already enjoys reading, have them read the classic works as well as biographies and their usual fiction books.

- Have one Saturday or Sunday be a device-free day. This one may be difficult at first. You may want to start with one day a month, depending on your family's device addiction.

- Start a family "pen pal" letter a month, where your child writes an actual letter and mails it to a family member. You will be shocked how they will actually come to love this, especially when the family member writes back! This will improve their handwriting, grammar, and communication skills, and who doesn't like to get a real letter in the mail?

What You Can Do:

- Get them books that work on and build their critical thinking. The Critical Thinking Company has tons of choices. They have books by age, by subject, and by grade. They also offer full curriculum packages if you really want to supplement your child's education.

- There are three books that we believe every child should read. All three of them are available on Amazon.com. You could also check your local library; they may have copies as well.
  1. *The Thinking Toolbox: Thirty-Five Lessons That Will Build Your Reasoning Skills*, by Nathaniel Bluedorn
  2. *The Fallacy Detective: Thirty-Eight Lessons on How to Recognize Bad Reasoning*, by Nathaniel Bluedorn
  3. *An Illustrated Book of Bad Arguments*, by Ali Almossawi

- Pick up old-fashioned crossword puzzle books or the Mensa books and do those together as a family one night. You could also use them on a driving trip to pass the time.

- If you have a creative child in the house, encourage them to paint, draw, sculpt, or write more.

What You Can Do:

- Spend a night playing board games or cards together. I know, it sounds so cheesy and old-fashioned, but we make a big deal out of it and our now-teenage children love this.

Below are a few suggestions. We have not played all of these games, so please review and decide if they are a good fit for your family. Always look for the "family" version if you have younger kids under 15 years old.

Monopoly	Double Ditto
Telestrations	Codenames
Life	Sequence
Punderdome	Spontuneous
Chinese Checkers	Spy Alley
Watch Ya' Mouth	Clue
Unstable Unicorns	5 Second Rule
Speed Charades	Taboo *for Kids*
I should have known that!	Risk

CHAPTER 14

Trust but Verify Is the Key

In closing, the most important piece of advice we can give you is this: If you are going to let your children have technology and play in the digital world, you must employ trust but verify. Hands-off parenting will not work and will only lead to disaster.

Trust but verify means you must sit down with your child and explain that you are going to allow them to have some access to the digital world and that you are going to trust that they will make wise decisions based on how they have been raised and the ongoing conversations you will be having, while at the same time deploying monitoring tools and ongoing parental guidance to verify everything is being used properly.

There is no single tool, device, app, or other gizmo that can adequately protect a child from the thousands of digital dangers that exist today.

As we mentioned in the introduction of the book, the best approach involves looking at the protection of your child like the layers of an onion. The more layers you have in place, the better the protection it will provide for your child.

Some tools are only good for social media, some are only good for phone apps, and some can only protect the device while it is at your house. Again, the best approach is to have multiple layers of protection.

We have tested many of the programs on the market today and have developed several best practice guides to cut through the confusion and help any parent implement the protection required for keeping their child safe online.

Trust but verify means installing monitoring software on devices, having parental controls, having ongoing conversations, as well as having other equipment (and settings) in place to protect your child. It may also mean not being the "cool" parent. Believe us when we say, "Trust but verify could save your child's life!"

It is better to be vaguely right than exactly wrong," –British philosopher and logician Carveth Read, 1898.

Warren Buffett has updated Mr. Read's quote for the twentieth century: *"It is better to be approximately right than precisely wrong."*

Now it's up to you!

With this book, we have provided a candid look at the online dangers your children face and the serious impacts they can have on their future. Even the parents who have grown up with technology know there is a problem with the incessant use of technology by both children and adults.

Now you face a decision that is entirely yours to make.

There is a version of a parable that is told by the Boy Scouts, Girl Scouts, every culture around the world, and within all denominations of religions throughout the world.

A version of this parable was even used by Toni Morrison, a 1993 Nobel Prize Winner, at her acceptance speech. The origins of the story are untraceable, yet the power and meaning of the story is universal.

Once there was a wise old man and a smart little boy. The boy was driven by a single desire, to expose the wise old man as a fool.

The smart boy had a plan.

He had captured a small and very fragile bird in the forest.

With the bird cupped in his hands, the boy's scheme was to approach the old man and ask him, "Old man, what do I have in my hands?" to which the wise old man would reply, "You have a bird, my son."

Then the boy would ask, "Old man, is the bird alive or is it dead?" If the old man replied that the bird was dead, the smart boy would open his hands and allow the bird to fly off back into the forest. But if the old man replied that the bird was alive, the smart boy would crush the bird to death. Then the boy would open his hands and say, "See, old man, the bird is dead!"

So it was, the smart boy went to the old man and said, "Old man, what do I have in my hands?"

The wise old man replied, "You have a bird, my son."

The boy grinned, sure that he was about to prove the old man a fool, and said, "Is the bird alive or is it dead?"

Whereupon the old man looked down at the boy sadly and replied, "The bird is in *your* hands, my son."

Having read this book, you now know that the digital world can have a very real and serious impact on your child's future. While still under *your* roof, with *your* financial support, the future and online fate of *your* child is in *your* hands.

You will need to decide what protections you put in place, what conversations you have, or if you will continue down the path we see many parents take.

Many parents take the parental path of least resistance, their hands thrown up in the air stating, "What's the use? They know more about technology than I do. They already have access, so it's too late. I can't do anything about what they do online, hopefully it will be OK."

If your child is still alive, it is never too late to begin or improve their online protection.

We have provided many tips and suggestions throughout the book. If you have not registered your book already, please do it now. Upon registration, you will get the Parenting Technology Toolkit, which contains valuable resources to help you protect your children online.

"It's not hard to make decisions once you know what your values are." –Roy E. Disney

Download The Parenting Technology Toolkit For FREE!

READ THIS FIRST

Just to say thanks for reading our book, we would like to give you The Parenting Technology Toolkit that contains additional resources to help you on your quest to protect your kids online absolutely FREE. *-Chris Good & Lisa Good*

To register your book go to:

www.AreYourKidsNakedOnline.com/registerbook

END NOTES

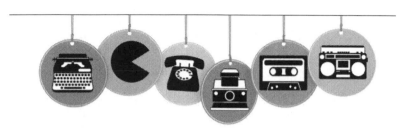

End Notes

1. Thesaurus.com, "Synonyms: Naked," Roget's 21st Century Thesaurus: thesaurus.com, 2013, https://www.thesaurus.com/browse/naked, accessed December 27, 2018.

2. Evan Andrews, "Who Invented the Internet?," A&E Television Networks, LLC: History.com, December 18, 2013, https://www.history.com/news/who-invented-the-internet, accessed December 27, 2018.

3. H. Hedegaard, M. Warner, and A.M. Miniño, "Drug Overdose Deaths in the United States, 1999–2016," NCHS Data Brief, no 294. Hyattsville, MD: National Center for Health Statistics, 2017, https://www.cdc.gov/nchs/data/databriefs/db294.pdf, accessed December 27, 2018.

4. The CDC Gateway Team, "Suicide Among Youth Tip Sheet," Centers for Disease Control and Prevention, https://www.cdc.gov/healthcommunication/toolstemplates/entertainmented/tips/SuicideYouth.html, accessed December 27, 2018.

5. Donald R. Lynam et al., "Project DARE: No Effects at 10-Year Follow-Up," Journal of Consulting and Clinical Psychology 67, no. 4 (August 1999): 590–593, http://citeseerx.ist.psu.edu/viewdoc/download?doi=10.1.1.501.4490&rep=rep1&type=pdf,accessed December 27, 2018.

Stephen J. Tripodi, Kimberly Bender, et al., "Interventions for Reducing Adolescent Alcohol Abuse: A Meta-Analytic Review," Archives of Pediatric and Adolescent Medicine, 164, no. 1 (January 2010): 85-91, doi: 10.1001/archpediatrics.2009.235, https://www.ncbi.nlm.nih.gov/pubmed/20048247, accessed December 27, 2018.

Steven L. West and Keri K O'Neal, "Project D.A.R.E. Outcome Effectiveness Revisited" American Journal of Public Health, 94, no. 6 (2004): 1027–1029, https://www.ncbi.nlm.nih.gov/pmc/articles/PMC1448384/, accessed December 27, 2018.

6. Ofir Turel, Qinghua He, Gui Xue, Lin Xiao, and Antoine Bechara, "Examination of Neural Systems Sub-Serving Facebook 'Addiction,'" Psychological Reports, 115, no. 3 (December 2014): 675–695, doi:10.2466/18.PR0.115c31z8, accessed December 27, 2018.

7. Bank of America, "Trends in Consumer Mobility Report 2015," Bank of America, 2015, https://promo.bankofamerica.com/mobilityreport/assets/images/2015-Trends-in-Consumer-Mobility-Report_FINAL.pdf, accessed December 27, 2018.

8. Mark Muro, Sifan Liu, et al., "Digitalization and the American Workforce," The Brookings Institution: Brookings.edu, November 2017, https://www.brookings.edu/research/digitalization-and-the-american-workforce/, accessed December 27, 2018.

9. Kristin MacLaughlin, "The Detrimental Effects of Pornography on Small Children," Content Watch Holdings, Inc: NetNanny.com, December 19, 2017, https://www.netnanny.com/blog/the-detrimental-effects-of-

pornography-on-small-children/, accessed December 27, 2018.

10. Brett Schetzsle, "Growing Up Online: What Kids Conceal," AO Kaspersky Lab: Kaspersky.com, April 6, 2016, https://kids.kaspersky.com/wp-content/uploads/2016/04/KL_Report_GUO_What_Kids_Conceal.pdf, accessed December 27, 2018.

11. S. Madigan, A. Ly, C.L. Rash, J. Van Ouytsel, and J.R. Temple, "Prevalence of Multiple Forms of Sexting Behavior Among Youth: A Systematic Review and Meta-Analysis," JAMA Pediatrics, 172, no. 4 (2018): 327–335, doi:10.1001/jamapediatrics.2017.5314, accessed December 27, 2018.

12. Facebook, "Community Standards Enforcement Report: Fake Accounts," Facebook.com, November 2018, https://transparency.facebook.com/community-standards-enforcement#fake-accounts, accessed December 27, 2018.

13. Cyrus Mistry, "All Types of Chromebooks for All Types of Learners," Google: Chromebooks for Education, January 24, 2018, https://blog.google/outreach-initiatives/education/all-types-chromebooks-all-types-learners/, accessed December 27, 2018.

14. Irwin Reyes, Primal Wijesekera, Joel Reardon, et al., "'Won't Somebody Think of the Children?' Examining COPPA Compliance at Scale," Proceedings on Privacy Enhancing Technologies, No. 3 (2018): 63–83. from doi:10.1515/popets-2018-0021, accessed December 27, 2018.

15. Google, "G Suite for Education Privacy Notice," Google for Education, No Date Listed, https://gsuite.google.com/intl/en/terms/education_privacy.html, accessed December 27, 2018.

16. Jonah Engel Bromwich, "Logan Paul, YouTube Star, Says Posting Video of Dead Body Was 'Misguided'," The New York Times Company: nytimes.com, January 2, 2018, https://www.nytimes.com/2018/01/02/business/

media/logan-paul-youtube.html, accessed December 27, 2018.

Abby Ohlheiser, "Logan Paul Promised a 'New Chapter' after Vlogging a Dead Body. Then, the YouTuber Tasered a Dead Rat," The Washington Post, February 9, 2018, https://www.washingtonpost.com/news/the-intersect/wp/2018/02/09/logan-paul-promised-a-new-chapter-after-vlogging-a-dead-body-then-the-youtuber-tasered-a-dead-rat/, accessed December 27, 2018.

Collette Reitz, "Here's How Logan Paul's Life Has Changed Since That Controversial Suicide Forest Video," Elite Daily, April 28, 2018, https://www.elitedaily.com/p/heres-how-logan-pauls-life-has-changed-since-that-controversial-suicide-forest-video-8787879, accessed December 27, 2018.

17. Jacqui Heinrich, "Deceptive Online Videos with Popular Kids Characters Hide Sinister Scenes," Cox Media Group: boston25news.com, March 19, 2018, https://www.boston25news.com/news/parents-disturbed-by-videos-featuring-violence-on-kids-app-1/718408215, accessed December 27, 2018.

18. Brigit Hennaman, "Mobile Kids: The Parent, the Child and the Smartphone," Neilsen: Neilsen Insights, February 28, 2017, https://www.nielsen.com/us/en/insights/news/2017/mobile-kids--the-parent-the-child-and-the-smartphone.html, accessed December 27, 2018.

19. Dana Page, "Mobile Fact Sheet," Pew Research Center: Internet & Technology, February 5, 2018, http://www.pewinternet.org/fact-sheet/mobile/, accessed December 27, 2018.

20. S. Madigan, A. Ly, C.L. Rash, J. Van Ouytsel, and J.R. Temple, "Prevalence of Multiple Forms of Sexting Behavior Among Youth: A Systematic Review and Meta-analysis," JAMA Pediatrics, 172, no. 4 (2018): 327–335, doi:10.1001/jamapediatrics.2017.5314, accessed December 27,

2018.

21. Erin Polka, "Teen Sexting," Public Health Post, 10-23-2018, https://www.publichealthpost.org/research/teen-sexting/, accessed December 27, 2018.

22. Pornhub, "2018 Year in Review," Pornhub: pornhub.com, 12-11-2018, https://www.pornhub.com/insights/2018-year-in-review, accessed December 27, 2018.

23. Sherri Gordon, "6 Things Teens Do Not Know About Sexting But Should," About, Inc. (Dotdash): verywellfamily.com, August 31, 2018, https://www.verywellfamily.com/things-teens-do-not-know-about-sexting-but-should-460654, accessed December 27, 2018.

24. Mark Wilson, "Bang With Friends Aims To Become Facebook's 'Klout for Banging,'" Fast Company, February 15, 2013, https://www.fastcompany.com/1671867/bang-with-friends-aims-to-become-facebooks-klout-for-banging, accessed December 27, 2018.

Mark Wilson, "Bang With Friends: The Beginning of a Sexual Revolution on Facebook," Fast Company, February 4, 2013, https://www.fastcompany.com/1671768/bang-with-friends-the-beginning-of-a-sexual-revolution-on-facebook, accessed December 27, 2018.

25. Iren, "DOWN Dating app review," AndroidAppsForMe.com, January 3, 2018, https://androidappsforme.com/down-dating-app-review/, accessed December 27, 2018.

26. Ryan Broderick, "9 Teenage Suicides in the Last Year Were Linked to Cyber-Bullying on Social Network Ask.fm," BuzzFeedNews.com, September 11, 2013, https://www.buzzfeednews.com/article/ryanhatesthis/a-ninth-teenager-since-last-september-has-committed-suicide, accessed December 27, 2018.

27. Thomas Brewster, "This $1 Billion App Can't 'Kik' Its Huge Child Exploitation Problem," Forbes Media LLC: Forbes.com, August 3, 2017, https://www.forbes.com/sites/thomasbrewster/2017/08/03/kik-has-a-massive-child-abuse-problem/, accessed December 27, 2018.

28. Tom Davis, "NJ Parents, Beware: Child Predators Use 19 'Apps' To Get Children," Patch Media: Patch.com, September 25, 2018, https://patch.com/new-jersey/pointpleasant/predators-nj-are-using-apps-get-children-authorities-say, accessed December 27, 2018.

29. Monica Anderson, Jingjing Jiang, "Teens, Social Media & Technology 2018," Pew Research Center, May 2018, http://assets.pewresearch.org/wp-content/uploads/sites/14/2018/05/31102617/PI_2018.05.31_TeensTech_FINAL.pdf, accessed December 27, 2018.

30. Lauren Reed, Richard Tolman, et al., "Gender matters: Experiences and Consequences of Digital Dating Abuse Victimization in Adolescent Dating Relationships," Journal of Adolescence, 59, (2017): 79-89, https://doi.org/10.1016/j.adolescence.2017.05.015, accessed December 27, 2018.

31. Department of Justice, "Man Who 'Sextorted' 12-Year-Old Girl Receives 10-Year Prison Sentence," Department of Justice, U.S. Attorney's Office, Northern District of Georgia, November 9, 2017, https://www.justice.gov/usao-ndga/pr/man-who-sextorted-12-year-old-girl-receives-10-year-prison-sentence, accessed December 27, 2018.

FBI.gov, "Cyberstalking: Two Federal Cases Illustrate the Consequences of Sextortion," FBI.gov, October 30, 2018, https://www.fbi.gov/news/stories/sentences-in-separate-cyberstalking-cases-103018, accessed December 27, 2018.

32. Sherri Gordon, "6 Things Teens Do Not Know About Sexting But Should," About, Inc. (Dotdash): verywellfamily.com, September 31, 2018, https://www.verywellfamily.com/things-teens-do-not-know-about-

sexting-but-should-460654, accessed December 27, 2018.

33. E. Englander, M. McCoy, "Sexting—Prevalence, Age, Sex, and Outcomes," JAMA Pediatrics, 172, no. 4 (2018): 317–318, doi:10.1001/jamapediatrics.2017.5682, accessed December 27, 2018.

34. Michael Seto, "Chapter 4: Internet-Facilitated Sexual Offending," Sex Offender Management Assessment and Planning Initiative: Office of Sex Offender Sentencing, Monitoring, Apprehending, Registering, and Tracking, March 2017, https://www.smart.gov/SOMAPI, accessed December 27, 2018.

35. Business Wire, "Digital Birth: Welcome to the Online World," BusinessWire.com, October 6, 2010, https://www.businesswire.com/news/home/20101006006722/en/Digital-Birth-Online-World, accessed December 27, 2018.

36. Christine Elgersma with Common Sense Media, "Parents, Here's the Truth about Online Predators," Turner Broadcasting System, Inc.: cnn.com, August 3, 2017, https://www.cnn.com/2017/08/03/health/online-predators-parents-partner/index.html, accessed December 27, 2018.

37. Kimberly J. Mitchell, Anna Segura, Lisa M. Jones, and Heather A. Turner, "Poly-Victimization and Peer Harassment Involvement in a Technological World," Journal of Interpersonal Violence, 33, no. 5 (March 2018): 762–788, doi:10.1177/0886260517744846, accessed December 27, 2018.

38. Mary Madden, Amanda Lenhart, et al., "Teens, Social Media, and Privacy," Pew Research Center: pewinternet.org, May 21, 2013, http://www.pewinternet.org/2013/05/21/teens-social-media-and-privacy/, accessed December 27, 2018.

39. Internet Watch Foundation, "Internet Watch Foundation, Annual

Report 2017," Internet Watch Foundation: iwf.org.uk, April 18, 2018, https://annualreport.iwf.org.uk/, accessed December 27, 2018.

40. DHS.gov, "Snapshot: DHS S&T and HSI Collaborate on Technologies to Save Children from Abuse and Exploitation," Department of Homeland Security Science and Technology, March 6, 2018, https://www.dhs.gov/science-and-technology/news/2018/03/06/snapshot-st-and-hsi-collaborate-technologies-save-children, accessed December 27, 2018.

41. The National Center for Missing and Exploited Children, "The Online Enticement of Children," NCMEC: missingkids.com, 2017, http://www.missingkids.com/content/dam/pdfs/ncmec-analysis/Online%20Enticement%20Pre-Travel.pdf, accessed December 27, 2018.

42. The NSOPW, "Raising Awareness About Sexual Abuse: Facts and Statistics," The NSOPW: nsopw.gov, No Date Listed, https://www.nsopw.gov/en-S/Education/FactsStatistics, accessed December 27, 2018.

43. Theesa.com, "U.S. Video Game Industry Generates $30.4 Billion in Revenue for 2016," ESA Entertainment Software Association, 1-19-2017, http://www.theesa.com/article/u-s-video-game-industry-generates-30-4-billion-revenue-2016/, accessed December 27, 2018.

44. James Batchelor, "Games industry generated $108.4bn in revenues in 2017," GamesIndustry.biz, January 31, 2018, https://www.gamesindustry.biz/articles/2018-01-31-games-industry-generated-usd108-4bn-in-revenues-in-2017, accessed December 27, 2018.

Superdataresearch.com, "Market Brief — 2017 Digital Games & Interactive Media Year in Review," SuperData Research Holdings, Inc., 2018, https://www.superdataresearch.com/market-data/market-brief-year-in-review/, accessed December 27, 2018.

45. David Lazarus, "Are Video Games Bad for Your Kids? Not So Much,

Experts Now Believe," LA Times: latimes.com, November 10, 2017, https://www.latimes.com/business/lazarus/la-fi-lazarus-video-games-parenting-20171110-story.html, accessed December 27, 2018.

46. Jihye Choi, et al., "Structural Alterations in the Prefrontal Cortex Mediate the Relationship Between Internet Gaming Disorder and Depressed Mood," Scientific Reports, 7, no. 1 (April 2017): 1245–1228, doi:10.1038/s41598-017-01275-5, accessed December 27, 2018.

Jory Deleuze, et al., "Established Risk Factors for Addiction Fail to Discriminate Between Healthy Gamers and Gamers Endorsing DSM-5 Internet Gaming Disorder," Journal of Behavioral Addictions, 6, no. 4 (2017): 516–524, accessed December 27, 2018.

Guangheng Dong, et al., "Gender-Related Differences in Neural Responses to Gaming Cues Before and After Gaming: Implications for Gender-Specific Vulnerabilities to Internet Gaming Disorder," Social Cognitive and Affective Neuroscience, 13, no. 11 (2018): 1203–1214, accessed December 27, 2018.

Daria J. Kuss, and Mark D. Griffiths, "Internet and Gaming Addiction: A Systematic Literature Review of Neuroimaging Studies," Brain Sciences, 2, no. 3 (September 5, 2012): 347–374, doi:10.3390/brainsci2030347, accessed December 27, 2018.

Daria J. Kuss, and Olatz Lopez-Fernandez, "Internet Addiction and Problematic Internet Use: A Systematic Review of Clinical Research," World Journal of Psychiatry, 6, no. 1 (March 22, 2016): 143–176, doi:10.5498/wjp.v6.i1.143, accessed December 27, 2018.

Daria J. Kuss et al. "Neurobiological Correlates in Internet Gaming Disorder: A Systematic Literature Review," Frontiers in Psychiatry, 9, no. 166 (May 8, 2018), doi:10.3389/fpsyt.2018.00166, accessed December 27, 2018.

Chang-Hyun Park, et al., "Alterations in the Connection Topology of Brain Structural Networks in Internet Gaming Addiction," Scientific Reports, 8, no. 1 (October 11, 2018): 15117, doi:10.1038/s41598-018-33324-y, accessed December 27, 2018.

Halley M. Pontes, "Investigating the Differential Effects of Social Networking Site Addiction and Internet Gaming Disorder on Psychological Health," Journal of Behavioral Addictions, 6, no. 4 (2017): 601-610, accessed December 27, 2018.

Aviv M. Weinstein, "An Update Overview on Brain Imaging Studies of Internet Gaming Disorder" Frontiers in Psychiatry, 8, no. 185 (September 29, 2017), doi:10.3389/fpsyt.2017.00185, accessed December 27, 2018.

Kristyn Zajac, et al., "Treatments for Internet Gaming Disorder and Internet Addiction: A Systematic Review," Psychology of Addictive Behaviors: Journal of the Society of Psychologists in Addictive Behaviors, 31, no. 8 (2017): 979–994, accessed December 27, 2018.

47. Hic, "Top Definition: Griefer," Urban Dictionary: urbandictionary.com, October 8, 2004, https://www.urbandictionary.com/define.php?term=griefer, accessed December 27, 2018.

48. Pornhub, "2018 Year in Review," Pornhub: pornhub.com, December 11, 2018, https://www.pornhub.com/insights/2018-year-in-review, accessed December 27, 2018.

49. Nick Paumgarten, "How Fortnite Captured Teens' Hearts and Minds," Condé Nast: newyorker.com, May 21, 2018, https://www.newyorker.com/magazine/2018/05/21/how-fortnite-captured-teens-hearts-and-minds, accessed December 27, 2018.

50. The National Institute of Mental Health, "Mental Health Information: Statistics: Suicide," The National Institute of Mental Health, May 2018,

https://www.nimh.nih.gov/health/statistics/suicide.shtml, accessed December 27, 2018.

51. Stopbullying.gov, "Facts About Bullying," Stopbullying.gov, September 28, 2017, https://www.stopbullying.gov/media/facts/index.html, accessed December 27, 2018.

52. Ditch the Label, "The Annual Bullying Survey 2017," Ditch the Label: ditchthelabel.org, July 2017, https://www.ditchthelabel.org/wp-content/uploads/2017/07/The-Annual-Bullying-Survey-2017-1.pdf, accessed December 27, 2018.

53. Daily Echo News, "Twynham School Pupil Leilani Clarke Took Her Own Life After Accessing Dark Web," Daily Echo News: bournemouthecho.co.uk/, July 19, 2018, https://www.bournemouthecho.co.uk/news/16366905.twynham-school-pupil-leilani-clarke-took-her-own-life-after-accessing-dark-web/, accessed December 27, 2018.

54. Crimesider Staff, "Texas Teen, Wife Accused of Hiring Hitman to Kill His Jeweler Father," CBS Interactive Inc.: cbsnews.com, May 31, 2018, https://www.cbsnews.com/news/texas-teen-wife-accused-of-hiring-hitman-to-kill-his-jeweler-father/, accessed December 27, 2018.

55. Pierluigi Paganini, "Hacking Communities in the Deep Web," Infosec Institute, May 15, 2018, https://resources.infosecinstitute.com/hacking-communities-in-the-deep-web/, accessed December 27, 2018.

56. Common Sense Media, "Landmark Report: U.S. Teens Use an Average of Nine Hours of Media Per Day, Tweens Use Six Hours," Common Sense Media, November 3, 2015, https://www.commonsensemedia.org/about-us/news/press-releases/landmark-report-us-teens-use-an-average-of-nine-hours-of-media-per-day, accessed December 27, 2018.

57. Nellie Bowles, "A Dark Consensus About Screens and Kids Begins to

Emerge in Silicon Valley," The New York Times: nytimes.com, October 26, 2018, https://www.nytimes.com/2018/10/26/style/phones-children-silicon-valley.html, accessed December 27, 2018.

BIBLIOGRAPHY

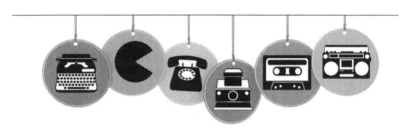

Bibliography

Anderson, Monica. "A Majority of Teens Have Experienced Some Form of Cyberbullying." Pew Research Center: Internet & Technology, September 27, 2018, http://www.pewinternet.org/2018/09/27/a-majority-of-teens-have-experienced-some-form-of-cyberbullying/, accessed December 27, 2018.

Anderson, Monica, Jingjing Jiang. "Teens, Social Media & Technology 2018." Pew Research Center, May 2018, http://assets.pewresearch.org/wp-content/uploads/sites/14/2018/05/31102617/PI_2018.05.31_TeensTech_FINAL.pdf, accessed December 27, 2018.

Andrews, Evan. "Who Invented the Internet?" A&E Television Networks, LLC: History.com, December 18, 2013, https://www.history.com/news/who-invented-the-internet, accessed December 27, 2018.

Bank of America. "Trends in Consumer Mobility Report 2015." Bank of America, 2015, https://promo.bankofamerica.com/mobilityreport/assets/images/2015-Trends-in-Consumer-Mobility-Report_FINAL.pdf, accessed

December 27, 2018.

Batchelor, James. "Games Industry Generated $108.4bn in Revenues in 2017." GamesIndustry.biz, January 31, 2018, https://www.gamesindustry.biz/articles/2018-01-31-games-industry-generated-usd108-4bn-in-revenues-in-2017, accessed December 27, 2018.

Bowles, Nellie. "A Dark Consensus About Screens and Kids Begins to Emerge in Silicon Valley." The New York Times: nytimes.com, October 26, 2018, https://www.nytimes.com/2018/10/26/style/phones-children-silicon-valley.html, accessed December 27, 2018.

Brewster, Thomas. "This $1 Billion App Can't 'Kik' Its Huge Child Exploitation Problem." Forbes Media LLC: Forbes.com, August 3, 2017, https://www.forbes.com/sites/thomasbrewster/2017/08/03/kik-has-a-massive-child-abuse-problem/, accessed December 27, 2018.

Broderick, Ryan. "9 Teenage Suicides in the Last Year Were Linked to Cyber-Bullying on Social Network Ask.fm." BuzzFeedNews.com, September 11, 2013, https://www.buzzfeednews.com/article/ryanhatesthis/a-ninth-teenager-since-last-september-has-committed-suicide, accessed December 27, 2018.

Bromwich, Jonah Engel. "Logan Paul, YouTube Star, Says Posting Video of Dead Body Was 'Misguided.'" The New York Times Company: nytimes.com, January 2, 2018, https://www.nytimes.com/2018/01/02/business/media/logan-paul-youtube.html, accessed December 27, 2018.

Business Wire. "Digital Birth: Welcome to the Online World." BusinessWire.com, October 6, 2010, https://www.businesswire.com/news/home/20101006006722/en/Digital-Birth-Online-World, accessed December 27, 2018.

The CDC Gateway Team. "Suicide Among Youth Tip Sheet." Centers for Disease

Control and Prevention, https://www.cdc.gov/healthcommunication/ toolstemplates/entertainmented/tips/SuicideYouth.html, accessed December 27, 2018.

Choi, Jihye, et al. "Structural Alterations in the Prefrontal Cortex Mediate the Relationship Between Internet Gaming Disorder and Depressed Mood." Scientific Reports, 7, no. 1 (April 28, 2017): 1245, doi:10.1038/s41598-017-01275-5, accessed December 27, 2018.

Common Sense Media. "Landmark Report: U.S. Teens Use an Average of Nine Hours of Media Per Day, Tweens Use Six Hours." Common Sense Media, November 3, 2015, https://www.commonsensemedia.org/about-us/news/press-releases/landmark-report-us-teens-use-an-average-of-nine-hours-of-media-per-day, accessed December 27, 2018.

Crimesider Staff. "Texas Teen, Wife Accused of Hiring Hitman to Kill His Jeweler Father." CBS Interactive Inc.: cbsnews.com, May 31, 2018, https://www.cbsnews.com/news/texas-teen-wife-accused-of-hiring-hitman-to-kill-his-jeweler-father/, accessed December 27, 2018.

Daily Echo News. "Twynham School Pupil Leilani Clarke Took Her Own Life After Accessing Dark Web." Daily Echo News: bournemouthecho.co.uk/, July 19, 2018, https://www.bournemouthecho.co.uk/news/16366905.twynham-school-pupil-leilani-clarke-took-her-own-life-after-accessing-dark-web/, accessed December 27, 2018.

Davis, Tom. "NJ Parents, Beware: Child Predators Use 19 'Apps' To Get Children." Patch Media: Patch.com, September 25, 2018, https://patch.com/new-jersey/pointpleasant/predators-nj-are-using-apps-get-children-authorities-say, accessed December 27, 2018.

Deleuze, Jory, et al. "Established Risk Factors for Addiction Fail to Discriminate Between Healthy Gamers and Gamers Endorsing DSM-5 Internet Gaming Disorder." Journal of Behavioral Addictions, 6, no. 4

(2017): 516–524, accessed December 27, 2018.

Department of Justice. "Man Who 'Sextorted' 12-Year-Old Girl Receives 10-Year Prison Sentence." Department of Justice, U.S. Attorney's Office, Northern District of Georgia, November 9, 2017, https://www.justice. gov/usao-ndga/pr/man-who-sextorted-12-year-old-girl-receives-10-year-prison-sentence, accessed December 27, 2018.

DHS.gov. "Snapshot: DHS S&T and HSI Collaborate on Technologies to Save Children from Abuse and Exploitation." Department of Homeland Security Science and Technology, March 6, 2018, https://www.dhs. gov/science-and-technology/news/2018/03/06/snapshot-st-and-hsi-collaborate-technologies-save-children, accessed December 27, 2018.

Ditch the Label. "The Annual Bullying Survey 2017." Ditch the Label: ditchthelabel.org, July 2017, https://www.ditchthelabel.org/wp-content/uploads/2017/07/The-Annual-Bullying-Survey-2017-1.pdf, accessed December 27, 2018.

Dong, Guangheng, et al. "Gender-Related Differences in Neural Responses to Gaming Cues Before and After Gaming: Implications for Gender-Specific Vulnerabilities to Internet Gaming Disorder." Social Cognitive and Affective Neuroscience, 13, 11 (2018): 1203–1214, accessed December 27, 2018.

Elgersma, Christine, with Common Sense Media. "Parents, Here's the Truth About Online Predators." Turner Broadcasting System, Inc.: cnn. com, August 3, 2017, https://www.cnn.com/2017/08/03/health/online-predators-parents-partner/index.html, accessed December 27, 2018.

Englander, E., McCoy M. "Sexting—Prevalence, Age, Sex, and Outcomes." JAMA Pediatrics, 172, no. 4 (2018): 317–318, doi:10.1001/jamapediatrics.2017.5682, accessed December 27, 2018.

Facebook. "Community Standards Enforcement Report: Fake Accounts." Facebook.com, November 2018, https://transparency.facebook.com/community-standards-enforcement#fake-accounts, accessed December 27, 2018.

FBI.gov. "Cyberstalking: Two Federal Cases Illustrate the Consequences of Sextortion." FBI.gov, October 30, 2018, https://www.fbi.gov/news/stories/sentences-in-separate-cyberstalking-cases-103018, accessed December 27, 2018.

Google. "G Suite for Education Privacy Notice." Google for Education, No Date Listed, https://gsuite.google.com/intl/en/terms/education_privacy.html, accessed December 27, 2018.

Gordon, Sherri. "6 Things Teens Do Not Know About Sexting But Should." About, Inc. (Dotdash): verywellfamily.com, August 31, 2018, https://www.verywellfamily.com/things-teens-do-not-know-about-sexting-but-should-460654, accessed December 27, 2018.

Hedegaard, H., Warner M, Miniño AM. "Drug Overdose Deaths in the United States, 1999–2016." NCHS Data Brief, no 294. Hyattsville, MD: National Center for Health Statistics, 2017, https://www.cdc.gov/nchs/data/databriefs/db294.pdf, accessed December 27, 2018.

Heinrich, Jacqui. "Deceptive Online Videos with Popular Kids Characters Hide Sinister Scenes." Cox Media Group: boston25news.com, March 19, 2018, https://www.boston25news.com/news/parents-disturbed-by-videos-featuring-violence-on-kids-app-1/718408215, accessed December 27, 2018.

Hennaman, Brigit. "Mobile Kids: The Parent, the Child and the Smartphone." Neilsen: Neilsen Insights, February 28, 2017, https://www.nielsen.com/us/en/insights/news/2017/mobile-kids--the-parent-the-child-and-the-smartphone.html, accessed December 27, 2018.

Hic. "Top Definition: Griefer." Urban Dictionary: urbandictionary.com, October 8, 2004, https://www.urbandictionary.com/define.php?term=griefer, accessed December 27, 2018.

Internet Watch Foundation. "Internet Watch Foundation, Annual Report 2017." Internet Watch Foundation: iwf.org.uk, April 18, 2018, https://annualreport.iwf.org.uk/, accessed December 27, 2018.

Iren. "DOWN Dating app review." AndroidAppsForMe.com, January 3, 2018, https://androidappsforme.com/down-dating-app-review/, accessed December 27, 2018.

The Jason Foundation. "Facts – Youth Suicide Statistics." The Jason Foundation, http://prp.jasonfoundation.com/facts/youth-suicide-statistics/, accessed December 27, 2018.

Kuss, Daria J., and Mark D. Griffiths. "Internet and Gaming Addiction: A Systematic Literature Review of Neuroimaging Studies." Brain Sciences, 2, no. 3 (September 5, 2012): 347–374, doi:10.3390/brainsci2030347, accessed December 27, 2018.

Kuss, Daria J., and Olatz Lopez-Fernandez. "Internet Addiction and Problematic Internet Use: A Systematic Review of Clinical Research." World Journal of Psychiatry, 6, no. 1 (March 22, 2016): 143–176, doi:10.5498/wjp.v6.i1.143, accessed December 27, 2018.

Kuss, Daria J., et al. "Neurobiological Correlates in Internet Gaming Disorder: A Systematic Literature Review." Frontiers in Psychiatry, 9, no. 166 (May 8, 2018), doi:10.3389/fpsyt.2018.00166, Accessed December 27, 2018.

Lazarus, David. "Are Video Games Bad for Your Kids? Not So Much, Experts Now Believe." LA Times: latimes.com, 11-10-2017, https://www.latimes.com/business/lazarus/la-fi-lazarus-video-games-parenting-20171110-

story.html, accessed December 27, 2018.

Lynam, Donald R., AM. "Project DARE: No Effects at 10-Year Follow-Up." Journal of Consulting and Clinical Psychology, 67, no. 4 (August 1999): 590–593, http://citeseerx.ist.psu.edu/viewdoc/download?doi=10.1.1.501. 4490&rep=rep1&type=pdf, accessed December 27, 2018.

MacLaughlin, Kristin. "The Detrimental Effects of Pornography on Small Children." Content Watch Holdings, Inc: NetNanny.com, December 19, 2017, https://www.netnanny.com/blog/the-detrimental-effects-of-pornography-on-small-children/, accessed December 27, 2018.

Madden, Mary, Amanda Lenhart, AM. "Teens, Social Media, and Privacy." Pew Research Center: pewinternet.org, May 21, 2013, http://www. pewinternet.org/2013/05/21/teens-social-media-and-privacy/, accessed December 27, 2018.

Madigan, S., Ly, A., Rash, C.L., Van Ouytsel, J., Temple, J.R. "Prevalence of Multiple Forms of Sexting Behavior Among Youth: A Systematic Review and Meta-Analysis." JAMA Pediatrics, 172, no. 4 (2018): 327–335, doi:10.1001/jamapediatrics.2017.5314, accessed December 27, 2018.

Mistry, Cyrus. "All Types of Chromebooks for All Types of Learners." Google: Chromebooks for Education, January 24, 2018, https://blog. google/outreach-initiatives/education/all-types-chromebooks-all-types-learners/, accessed December 27, 2018.

Mitchell, Kimberly J., Anna Segura, Lisa M. Jones, and Heather A. Turner. "Poly-Victimization and Peer Harassment Involvement in a Technological World." Journal of Interpersonal Violence 33, no. 5 (March 2018): 762–788, doi:10.1177/0886260517744846, accessed December 27, 2018.

Muro, Mark, Sifan Liu, AM. "Digitalization and the American Workforce." The Brookings Institution: Brookings.edu, November 2017, https://www.

brookings.edu/research/digitalization-and-the-american-workforce/, accessed December 27, 2018.

The National Center for Missing and Exploited Children, "The Online Enticement of Children," NCMEC: missingkids.com, 2017, http://www.missingkids.com/content/dam/pdfs/ncmec-analysis/Online%20 Enticement%20Pre-Travel.pdf, accessed December 27, 2018.

The National Institute of Mental Health. "Mental Health Information: Statistics: Suicide." The National Institute of Mental Health, May 2018, https://www.nimh.nih.gov/health/statistics/suicide.shtml, accessed December 27, 2018.

The National Institute on Drug Abuse Blog Team. "Drug Overdoses in Youth." Drugs & Health Blog, National Institute on Drug Abuse, https://teens.drugabuse.gov/drug-facts/drug-overdoses-youth, Accessed December 27, 2018

The NSOPW. "Raising Awareness About Sexual Abuse: Facts and Statistics." The NSOPW: nsopw.gov, No Date Listed, https://www.nsopw.gov/en-S/ Education/FactsStatistics, accessed December 27, 2018.

Ohlheiser, Abby. "Logan Paul Promised a 'New Chapter' After Vlogging a Dead Body. Then, the YouTuber Tasered a Dead Rat." The Washington Post, February 9, 2018, https://www.washingtonpost.com/news/the-intersect/wp/2018/02/09/logan-paul-promised-a-new-chapter-after-vlogging-a-dead-body-then-the-youtuber-tasered-a-dead-rat/, accessed December 27, 2018.

Paganini, Pierluigi. "Hacking Communities in the Deep Web." Infosec Institute, May 15, 2018, https://resources.infosecinstitute.com/hacking-communities-in-the-deep-web/, accessed December 27, 2018.

Page, Dana. "Mobile Fact Sheet," Pew Research Center: Internet &

Technology, February 5, 2018, http://www.pewinternet.org/fact-sheet/mobile/, accessed December 27, 2018.

Park, Chang-Hyun, et al. "Alterations in the Connection Topology of Brain Structural Networks in Internet Gaming Addiction." Scientific Reports 8, no. 1 (October 11, 2018): 15117, doi:10.1038/s41598-018-33324-y, accessed December 27, 2018.

Paumgarten, Nick. "How Fortnite Captured Teens' Hearts and Minds," Condé Nast: newyorker.com, May 21, 2018, https://www.newyorker.com/magazine/2018/05/21/how-fortnite-captured-teens-hearts-and-minds, accessed December 27, 2018.

Polka, Erin. "Teen Sexting." Public Health Post, October 23, 2018, https://www.publichealthpost.org/research/teen-sexting/, accessed December 27, 2018.

Pontes, Halley M. "Investigating the Differential Effects of Social Networking Site Addiction and Internet Gaming Disorder on Psychological Health." Journal of Behavioral Addictions 6, no. 4 (2017): 601–610, accessed December 27, 2018.

Pornhub. "2018 Year in Review," Pornhub: pornhub.com, 12-11-2018, https://www.pornhub.com/insights/2018-year-in-review, accessed December 27, 2018.

Reed, Lauren, Richard Tolman AM. "Gender Matters: Experiences and Consequences of Digital Dating Abuse Victimization in Adolescent Dating Relationships." Journal of Adolescence, ISSN: 1095-9254, 59 (2017): 79–89, https://doi.org/10.1016/j.adolescence.2017.05.015, accessed December 27, 2018.

Reitz, Collette. "Here's How Logan Paul's Life Has Changed Since That Controversial Suicide Forest Video." Elite Daily, April 28, 2018, https://

www.elitedaily.com/p/heres-how-logan-pauls-life-has-changed-since-that-controversial-suicide-forest-video-8787879, accessed December 27, 2018.

Reyes, Irwin, Primal Wijesekera, Joel Reardon, et al. 2018. "'Won't Somebody Think of the Children?' Examining COPPA Compliance at Scale." Proceedings on Privacy Enhancing Technologies 3 (2018): 63–83, from doi:10.1515/popets-2018-0021, accessed December 27, 2018.

Root, Elena, Bogdan Melnykov. "Malware Displaying Porn Ads Discovered in Game Apps on Google Play." Check Point Research: Check Point Software Technologies LTD, 2018, https://research.checkpoint.com/malware-displaying-porn-ads-discovered-in-game-apps-on-google-play/, accessed December 27, 2018.

Schetzsle, Brett. "Growing Up Online: What Kids Conceal." AO Kaspersky Lab: Kaspersky.com, April 6, 2016, https://kids.kaspersky.com/wp-content/uploads/2016/04/KL_Report_GUO_What_Kids_Conceal.pdf, accessed December 27, 2018.

Seto, Michael. "Chapter 4: Internet-Facilitated Sexual Offending." Sex Offender Management Assessment and Planning Initiative: Office of Sex Offender Sentencing, Monitoring, Apprehending, Registering, and Tracking, March 2017, https://www.smart.gov/SOMAPI, accessed December 27, 2018.

Stopbullying.gov. "Facts About Bullying." Stopbullying.gov, September 28, 2017, https://www.stopbullying.gov/media/facts/index.html, accessed December 27, 2018.

Superdataresearch.com. "Market Brief—2017 Digital Games & Interactive Media Year in Review." SuperData Research Holdings, Inc., 2018, https://www.superdataresearch.com/market-data/market-brief-year-in-review/, accessed December 27, 2018.

Theesa.com. "U.S. Video Game Industry Generates $30.4 Billion in Revenue for 2016." ESA Entertainment Software Association, January 19, 2017, http://www.theesa.com/article/u-s-video-game-industry-generates-30-4-billion-revenue-2016/, accessed December 27, 2018.

Thesaurus.com. "Synonyms: Naked," Roget's 21st Century Thesaurus: thesaurus.com, 2013, https://www.thesaurus.com/browse/naked, accessed December 27, 2018.

Tripodi, Stephen J., Kimberly Bender, AM. "Interventions for Reducing Adolescent Alcohol Abuse: A Meta-Analytic Review." Archives of Pediatric Adolescent Medicine 164, no. 1 (January 2010): 85–91, doi: 10.1001/archpediatrics.2009.235, Jan 2010, https://www.ncbi.nlm.nih.gov/pubmed/20048247, accessed December 27, 2018.

Turel, Ofir, Qinghua He, Gui Xue, Lin Xiao, and Antoine Bechara. "Examination of Neural Systems Sub-Serving Facebook 'Addiction.'" Psychological Reports 115, no. 3 (December 2014): 675–695, doi:10.2466/18.PR0.115c31z8, accessed December 27, 2018.

Weinstein, Aviv M. "An Update Overview on Brain Imaging Studies of Internet Gaming Disorder." Frontiers in Psychiatry 8, no. 185 (September 29, 2017), doi:10.3389/fpsyt.2017.00185, accessed December 27, 2018.

West, Steven L. and Keri K. O'Neal. "Project D.A.R.E. Outcome Effectiveness Revisited." American Journal of Public Health 94, no. 6 (2004): 1027–1029, https://www.ncbi.nlm.nih.gov/pmc/articles/PMC1448384/, accessed December 27, 2018.

Wilson, Mark. "Bang With Friends Aims to Become Facebook's 'Klout for Banging.'" Fast Company, February 15, 2013, https://www.fastcompany.com/1671867/bang-with-friends-aims-to-become-facebooks-klout-for-banging, accessed December 27, 2018.

Wilson, Mark. "Bang With Friends: The Beginning of a Sexual Revolution on Facebook." Fast Company, February 4, 2013, https://www.fastcompany.com/1671768/bang-with-friends-the-beginning-of-a-sexual-revolution-on-facebook, accessed December 27, 2018.

Zajac, Kristyn, et al. "Treatments for Internet Gaming Disorder and Internet Addiction: A Systematic Review." Psychology of Addictive Behaviors: Journal of the Society of Psychologists in Addictive Behaviors 31, no. 8 (2017): 979–994, accessed December 27, 2018.

Zimmerman, Kim Ann, Jesse Emspak. "Internet History Timeline: ARPANET to the World Wide Web." Live Science, June 27, 2017, https://www.livescience.com/20727-internet-history.html, accessed December 27, 2018.

35639359R00119

Made in the USA
Middletown, DE
09 February 2019